CG CHALLENGE

MACHINEFLESH

CG Challenge organizers

Leigh van der Byl and Leonard Teo

Editor

Daniel Wade

Published
by

Ballistic Publishing

Publishers of digital works for the digital world

Aldgate Valley Rd
Mylor SA 5153
Australia

www.BallisticPublishing.com

Correspondence:
info@BallisticPublishing.com

First Edition published in Australia 2005 by Ballistic Publishing

Softcover Edition ISBN 1-921002-09-3

Editor
Daniel Wade

CG Challenge organizers
Leonard Teo, Leigh van der Byl

Art Director
Mark Snoswell

Design & Image Processing
Stuart Colafella

Printing and binding
Everbest Printing (China)
www.everbest.com

Subsidiaries
CGNetworks: www.CGNetworks.com
CGTalk: www.CGTalk.com

Affiliate
cgCharacter: www.cgCharacter.com

Cover image credits

Krishnamurti M. Costa
California, USA
[Front cover: CGChallenge Machineflesh]

Cybernetic Basketball Player
bOne, FRANCE
[Back cover: CGChallenge Machineflesh]

MACHINEFLESH

Winner 3D

Winner
Krishnamurti M. Costa (Antropus)
California, USA

Page 8

Winner 2D

Winner
Daryl Mandryk (Blackarts)
Electronic Arts, Vancouver, CANADA

Page 38

Runners-up 3D

1st Runner-up
Greg Petchkovsky (gjpetch)
Sydney, AUSTRALIA

Page 16

2nd Runner-up
Ila Soleimani (ila_Solomon)
Tehran, IRAN

Page 24

3rd Runner-up
Bernardo Delgado (Bernardo D)
Colima, MEXICO

Page 30

Runners-up 2D

1st Runner-up
Jeff Rey (Goli)
FRANCE

Page 44

2nd Runner-up
Damian Bajowski
(mime_ evermotion)
Evermotion, POLAND

Page 50

3rd Runner-up
Francis Tsai (francis001)
Sammy Studios
California, USA

Page 54

Gallery of honourable mentions Page 60

Leonard Teo | Founder,
CGNetworks and CGTalk
Managing Director, Ballistic Media

Challenge yourself

An innate desire within humans makes us want to challenge ourselves. In sports, exploration, education and other competitive endeavours, we seek that adrenaline rush that pushes us beyond our capabilities. Whether it is the thrill of the contest, bettering our skills or attempting to prove our mettle to peers, we have shown that we like challenges, and we love beating the odds. The CG Challenges, run on CGNetworks.com and its forums CGTalk.com, are testament to this desire to achieve. With each Challenge now attracting over 2,000 contestants worldwide, and over 10,000 images uploaded, it has become a mammoth competition for digital artists.

The Challenges began in true grassroots fashion. In 2002, members of the CGTalk.com community began 'challenging' each other to specific tasks—usually modelling 3D characters. The whole concept behind these 'challenges' was to learn from each other. Each participant had to show their Work-In-Progress (WIP) screengrabs, exposing their techniques to other challengers for improving skills. Specific themes were set up for artists to stretch their imagination and creativity.

Absolutely no-one was prepared for the excitement that would follow, when many production artists participated in the Challenge, creating awesome works of art that would inspire an entire community, and spawn the start of the world's largest online digital art contests. Over a period of two years, the CGTalk community has been host to 15 CG Challenges. Themes have included: Pirates, Post-Apocalypse, Gods and Demons, Beasts of Burden, Twisted Extreme Sports, Living Toons, Awkward Moments, Races of Middle Earth, Hapless Heroes and more.

Sadly, much of the artwork and records of these Challenges have been lost due to the temporal nature of the Web. With the Challenges running primarily on the CGTalk forums, artists hosted their artwork on personal websites. As these files were removed, so were all formal records of their existence and participation in the Challenges. Furthermore, the large number of participants, sponsors and jury members were too much for our volunteer crew of moderators to manage. We needed to take the CG Challenge to the next level.

CG Challenge XIV: Alienware was the breakthrough Challenge which employed strict rules for participants, formal entry procedures, and image upload/hosting facilities. Raising the bar further, we followed up with CG Challenge XV: Machineflesh, which offered the largest pool of prizes ever awarded. The "Machineflesh" theme challenged artists to depict mechanically altered and enhanced organic life in a macabre mix of sci-fi and horror. With prizes from Boxx Technologies, Wacom, NVIDIA, Discreet, The Gnomon Workshop and Ballistic Publishing totalling over US$20,000, the Challenge broke all records.

Despite the massive popularity and success of the Machineflesh Challenge, its sheer scale caused immense problems once again in its administration. With server bandwidth and storage costs ballooning due to over usage, and the amount of staff resources allocated to administering and running the Challenge, it became clear that we needed to raise the CG Challenges to another level and find ways to fund them. We knew that much of the artwork created in the Challenges were print-worthy, and wanted to document the making-of's in a medium that artists could refer to in years to come. The Web, being a temporal medium, would not be able to act as a persistent record of these Challenges.

In November 2004, we raised the idea of creating a Machineflesh Challenge book to the finalists of the Challenge. Over 99% of the respondents voted that we should create the book! We found that many contestants not only wanted a lasting record of the Challenges, but also wanted to contribute to help finance and continue the CG Challenges. It is important to note that CG Challenge book proceeds will go towards financing the Challenges, as we found that running contests of this size for free to the community is absurdly expensive.

The result is a stunning mix of documented techniques and gallery material in this Machineflesh book—the first in a series of CG Challenge books that will document the online contests. It has been a long, arduous road to this point and we're extremely proud that the Challenges now have a means of being recorded in a static medium for years to come. We're also very excited about the next CG Challenge publication, which will document the CG Challenge XVI: Grand Space Opera.

It is our sincere hope that you will find the works presented in this Machineflesh book educational and inspirational, and that you'll join us in our online CG Challenges!

Thank you

The following people were instrumental in the proliferation and development of the CG Challenges:

• Tito Belgrave, Leigh van der Byl, Alex Alvarez, Robert Mibus, Bonnie Kain, Travis Bourbeau, and the CGTalk Mod Crew.

To the Ballistic Publishing crew, for once again defying the odds:

• Mark Snoswell, Daniel P Wade, Stuart Colafella, Garth Hammet, Helen Snoswell, and Eric Dechegne.

PONSORS

GNetworks thanks the sponsors for their participation in the Machineflesh Challenge:

oxx Technologies - www.boxxtech.com   The Gnomon Workshop - www.thegnomonworkshop.com
VIDIA - www.nvidia.com   Wacom - www.wacom.com
screet - www.discreet.com   Ballistic Publishing - www.BallisticPublishing.com

CGNetworks.com :: CGTalk.com :: Ballistic Publishing.com :: EXPOSÉ 1 :: EXPOSÉ 2

CGNetworks.com
Creative Computer Graphics & Visual Effects

Welcome to CGNetworks.com,
the premier website for computer graphic arts.

Citizens: 128522, Threads: 175409, Posts: 1692330

LOGIN & REGISTER

- Search CGNetworks -

NEWS   ARTICLES   GALLERY   CGTALK   CGFILMS   CHALLENGES   NEWSLETTER   ABOUT

CHALLENGES

- ABOUT CGN CHALLENGES
- GRAND SPACE OPERA
- MACHINEFLESH - ARCHIVE
- CHALLENGE WINNERS
- INSTRUCTIONS
- PRIZES & SPONSORS
- VIEW ALL ENTRIES
- ENTRIES FORUM (2D)
- ENTRIES FORUM (3D)
- ALIENWARE - ARCHIVE

MachineFlesh Sponsors
- Boxx Technologies
- Wacom
- NVIDIA
- Discreet
- The Gnomon Workshop
- Ballistic Publishing

CGNetworks is proud to present the Machineflesh Challenge (CG Challenge XV),
16 March - 18 June 2004, sponsored by Boxx Technologies, Wacom, NVIDIA,
Discreet, The Gnomon Workshop and Ballistic Publishing.

Combining two popular themes (characters and machines), contestants were tasked to
create an image depicting a mechanically altered or enhanced organic lifeform. This
fifteenth challenge run by CGNetworks received over 1400 entries in the 3D category
and over 700 2D entries, making it almost twice as large as the previously run
challenge, and setting the record as the largest online art contest ever run!

Having said that, the voting process was quite a large undertaking, and the time has
finally come to announce who will walk away with those incredible prizes! CGNetworks
proudly congratulates all winners of the MachineFlesh Challenge!

Winning Results - 3D

Grand Prize Winner

Runners-Up

Greg
Petchkovsky
(gjpetch)
First Runner-Up

Leigh van der Byl
CGTalk Manager

Mid-February 2004: The enormous beast that was the Alienware Challenge had been and gone, leaving CGNetworks servers heaving and groaning in the wake of the onslaught of Challenge entries, and the moderators on CGTalk with the ever-taxing dilemma of deciding on a new Challenge topic. The phenomenal success of the previous Challenge had set a precedent. As web-based contests go, it had been positively gargantuan. Always pushing the envelope, the next one had to be even bigger. We needed something huge, something fantastic, and above all, something cool to top it.

The CGTalk moderator's forum was abuzz. Amid the brainstorming of the minds that had already conceived of space pirates, beasts of burden, wacky sports, alien worlds, gods and monsters and various other themes in the previous fourteen Challenges, I tossed the word "machineflesh" into the mix, hoping to steer the fervent discussion into a mechanical direction. Characters and machines—probably two of the most popular digital elements that we see daily on the forums—were an ideal combination, with a wide variety of possible interpretations, from macabre and grotesque to comical or absurd. It was twisted and cool. It was bound to have a wide appeal.

Of course, in the interests of preventing a potential testosterone-enriched overload of bikini-clad cyber-babes with oversized guns for arms, the carefully constructed Challenge guidelines encouraged artists to be imaginative with their concepts. Instead of sticking to old clichéd ideas and imagery, we asked artists to exercise their brains. We stressed the idea that the mechanical parts should serve some specific purpose, whether for combat, medical, labour or even punishment. These guidelines and stipulations were drawn up, an impressive and highly desirable selection of prizes were organised, and the Challenge was launched in March. The challengers had three months to conceptualize, create and deliver their "Machineflesh" progeny. Show us something cool.

The response was overwhelming. The flood of entries and ideas spawned over 2,000 challenge threads on the CGTalk forums spread over both 2D and 3D categories—a writhing, frenzied mass of concepts and fabulous digital art. Flesh was fused with steel, wiring, and bizarre contraptions to create a wide array of outlandish biotechnological super-creatures. A pixelated and

As always the ever-present camaraderie among challengers provided a platform for them to share insight, critique and good old-fashioned support for fellow contestants. These Challenges are not just about creating inspiring artwork, but about learning and developing one's skills and imagination, and among the hundreds of bouncing and "buttrocking" smileys, a glut of thoughts and techniques were shared for all.

As is to be expected in a Challenge of such proportions, Machineflesh presented its own set of idiosyncratic teething issues and frustrations. This being the second Challenge that we hosted, it was inevitable that we'd encounter various snags, abuse of the hosting service, and minor annoyances along the way. The wearying task of fielding numerous daily queries, removing sneakily submitted renders of cars and other non-Challenge images from the servers, and addressing technical issues is never an easy one, although we were fortunately spared from catastrophic mishaps or dilemmas.

While this challenge certainly had its share of artists who didn't really follow (or by some appearances, even read) the guidelines or fully exercise their imaginations (large-breasted robots with eye lasers, anyone?), as well as artists who disappointingly failed to submit all their required milestones, the Challenge was nevertheless a resounding success with a high volume of excellent artwork presented when the date of final delivery arrived. Artistic imagination and diligence had prevailed, and CG Challenge XV: Machineflesh came grinding to a halt. The following two weeks of judging (both from the public as well as a private jury of artists and sponsors) concluded and rewarded the top artists in a Challenge that saw 41,053 comments and posts from participating artists and supporters, over 7,000 uploaded milestone images, and a grand total of 2,174 challengers.

Since our Challenges have grown exponentially over the last two years, I'm sure we can look forward to something of positively epic proportions in the future.

Krishnamurti M. Costa

Winner

Machineflesh 3D

My main idea was to create something with high contrasts between different meanings. I created my sketch using no references. After the completion of the sketch, I started to research references for anatomy, like photos of pregnant women, footage from horror movies, umbilical cords, backgrounds and a lot of works from digital and traditional artists. Themes I tried to feature in my work include life and death, confinement and freedom, beauty and ugliness, woman and man, machine and flesh, mother and son. Each element in this piece has symbolic meaning that fits in with my original idea. Elements like the object on the Mother-machine's chin are a reference to the ancient pharaohs. The beast is a reference to the esfinge controlled by the "pharaoh". The monolith represents fire and water. Life is the fire, and the imminent death of both beings is represented by the rain. The "robot-pregnant" is like an Amazon warrior with visual reference to Medusa. You'll also notice that the beast can't see his mother's face, because he's in a submissive pose—he can try, but he will never see his mother's face.

Quick and dirty sketch

I started with a quick sketch using pen on paper. I spent some time thinking about the Challenge subject and trying to keep my mind free while I drew some free forms.

Second and final sketch

The next step was to create another sketch as a cleanup of my previous one where I added new details and better definition of the style that I decided to follow. Here, I had an approximate idea about the amount of details that I had to create to complete this project.

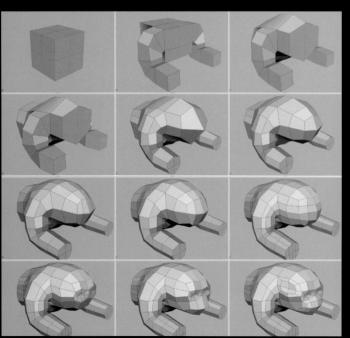

Modeling

For modeling I used Maya with CPS and MJPolyTools scripts. Both models ("Mother-machine" and "Homo-aeternus?") I created using the box-modeling technique. For the beast, I used a relatively dense mesh as a base for the final details. I exported the meshes from Maya to ZBrush (in .obj format), and used ZBrush to subdivide and add details to the beast and also to add and extract details (displacement maps) from Mother-machine's parts as a base for textures. To illustrate my workflow I've created a models sessions like in this image.

Appealing

For the Mother-machine I used a mostly mechanical approach keeping in mind the sensual forms of a real woman and the beauty of a pregnancy. I tried to make not only a robot, but a robot with a kind of almost-erotic "soul". I tried different edge loops to make the form fluid and also to make it easy to add new details to the head, breasts and belly.

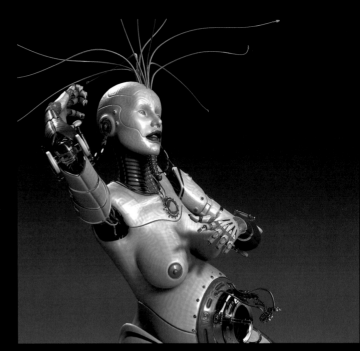

Secondary elements

I also created simple objects in Maya, exported to ZBrush and painted details such as the mountains and the monolith. My first intention was to use very complex models as a base for displacement maps applied over low-poly meshes in Maya. To avoid problems due to the complexity of the scene, I opted to use meshes with enough polygons to add a part of the details and texture maps to complete the final detailing.

UV mapping

For the textures, I first used Maya for the creation of the UVs layout and exported the plain maps to Photoshop. Using just a few pieces makes everything easier if you are planning to visualize and paint the maps using Photoshop.

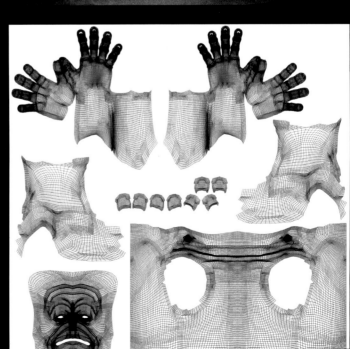

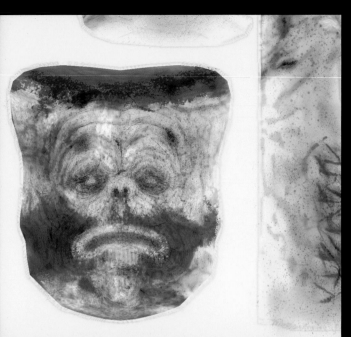

Textures

All the textures were painted by hand using Photoshop and ZBrush. I used color, ambient, specular, reflection and bump maps for every object in my scene.

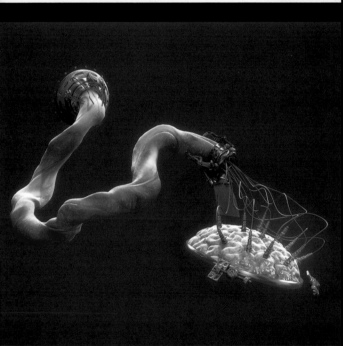

Maya to ZBrush to Maya

To correct some parts of the texture and to add more details, I exported .obj files to ZBrush again. Objects like the umbilical cord, the brain and the mountains were entirely painted inside ZBrush and the maps exported again to render in Maya.

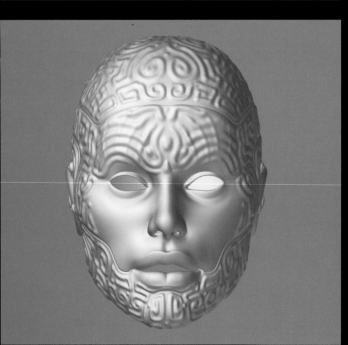

Displacement maps as bump maps

I also used ZBrush to export displacement maps as a base for bump and color maps, used over the Mother-machine's "skin". To do this, I just imported the low resolution models in ZBrush, subdivided several times, added lots of details and exported the displacement maps. Instead of using these maps as displacement maps I just used them in the color and bump maps.

Woman in ZBrush

Every piece of the Mother-machine had the same treatment: Low-poly > subD > Sculpting > Displacement map export > Connection into Maya's Shader Network > Render.

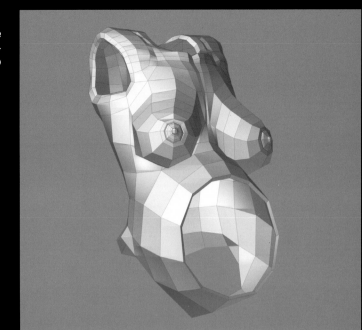

ZBrush's Cavity shader exported as maps

The background was also created and painted in ZBrush. To add more details and to create a dirty aspect, I used ZBrush's Cavity shader. To export this effect as a map I just used the displacement map as an alpha map, filled the screen, rendered and finally I exported the rendered image as a texture.

Composition

Another important step in my work is the composition. I'm always trying to work with a good composition to give my work good balance, rhythm, contrast and movement. I used a simple composition for this project, while trying to make it work within my intention.

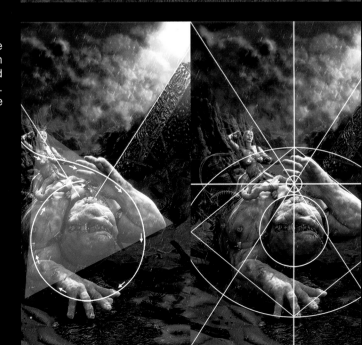

Simulated sub surface scattering (SSS)

I used some ramp and layered shaders in Maya to simulate a little bit of Subsurface Scattering and fresnel. Together I used bump, color, incandescence and specular maps to add the final details in the main characters. The map's resolution have between 600 x 600 and 3,200 x 3,200 pixels all in BOT format to render faster and use less memory in Maya.

Simulated GI Light

For the lighting, I used just Maya's default spots (49), omni (4) and area (2, just for reflections/speculars). I created a spherical dome with very attenuated spot lights on the bottom and strongest ones on top. After, I added the key lights using omnis to add some cool reflections/speculars I used area lights producing no light. I optimized the shadow map sizes to be sure that my computer could drive it and to make the render time faster.

Rendering in layers

For the final render, I deleted all the polygons that do not appear in the final render, trying to optimize the general size of my scene when loaded. I used two passes for the final render. The first one included all the objects in the foreground: main characters, background, grass and debris. The second pass was just for the mountains and lake. I used the default Maya render with raytrace turned on, for general reflections. For the final two passes, I used Maya's render by command line, to have more available RAM to handle my scene.

Post-proccessing

For the composition of my two-layer render I used Photoshop. I painted the clouds in Photoshop, creating and using some custom brushes. For the rain, I created a blank layer with noise effect applied. I used Blur > Gaussian Blur to reduce the grained aspect a little bit, then I used the Blur > Motion blur effect to add direction for the rain drops. I used Screen mode for this layer to multiply the rain effect over the original image. I added three more layers with different rain drop angles and different opacity levels, aiming for a more natural feeling. To add a little bit more of SSS effect in some parts, like in the beast's hands, I created another layer and painted over the desired parts with red/orange then I used a Color Dodge layer multiplier reducing the general opacity to something very subtle. To include some glow, I used a copy of the original image pre-composed, used Levels to make a high contrast image again, Gaussian Blur and Screen as a layer blend mode.

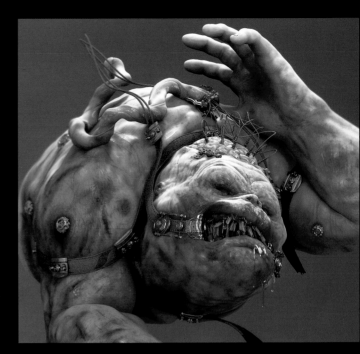

3D as art

I tried to create an almost "3D painting". I just love the art of old masters like Rembrandt, Caravaggio, Michellangelo, DaVinci, and Velazquez among others. They produced very expressive works playing with the lighting, composition, theatrical poses and a lot of contrasts (baroques). Everything was done by hand. I like the idea of using no plug-ins or ready-made textures to do my work. It's my personal style to approach from a traditional art perspective in CG. I can learn a lot more by doing everything myself, using no plug-ins. Even for lighting, I prefer to create my own setup because I believe I have much more liberty to create and fake effects, to "paint with lights", and to add a more dramatic feeling to my work. Here you can see one test that I did using a monochromatic approach just to check if the light of my scene will work.

Invisible details

Some parts of my work didn't appear in my final composition such as the extra details that I added to the Mother-machine. Sometimes you have to sacrifice part of your work to make the final piece more appealing. In any case, it was amazing to learn while I was working hard on small details like you can see here.

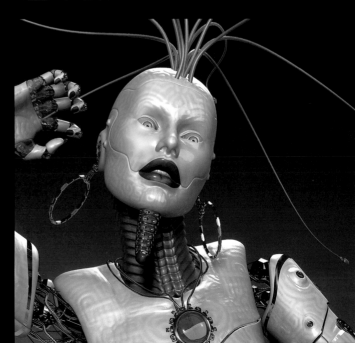

Greg Petchkovsky

Runner Up

Machineflesh 3D

I started doing 3D as a hobby about six years ago. Then, without any professional experience or 3D education I was somehow lucky enough to get a job in 3D at Animal Logic, where I have been working for almost three years now. I've always had an interest in visual arts, special effects and animation; I enjoy sculpture and drawing and my specialty in 3D is modeling. For the Machineflesh Challenge I drew ideas for the character from many different sources. The base ideas came from looking through my old sketchbook, and combining interesting features from my doodling. I also looked at a lot of reference from film and TV, as well as real-world machinery and wildlife photography. A lot of ideas and influences went into the image—some you may not notice. I gave him a subtle double iris in each eye, the idea being that he looks more frightening if you can't tell which direction he's looking. He also has a set of mechanical arms in his back holding his reins. My thinking was that the artificial intelligence behind his mechanical parts can't directly influence what he does, but has found this unusual workaround. Another source of ideas was classical mythology. I thought of the mechanical legs as a bit like the goat legs of mythological figures such as Pan and Puck.

Inspiration

I drew ideas for the character from many different sources. The base ideas came from looking through my old sketchbook, and combining interesting features from my doodling. I also looked at a lot of reference from film and TV as well as real-world machinery and wildlife photography. Thinking about favorite fictional characters such as Frankenstein's monster, Gollum, the Hunchback of Notre Dame, King Kong, the Iron Giant and so on made me want to make my character a sympathetic monster—hopefully this comes through in the final image.

Form and function

Most of my ideas were improvised while working in 3D, rather than while sketching. I really enjoyed adding small details for the viewer to discover. Part of the mechanism in the ankle is a bike chain. A tiny amount of smoke is coming out of the mechanism in his back. He has a gold tooth, and he has little pimples on his shoulders.

Details

I gave the character as many incidental and unusual details as I could think of, in an attempt to give the picture a sense of authenticity. He has a tattoo of a tree curling around his arm with a root reaching down each of his fingers, and a tattoo of a cog shape to reflect the theme of the challenge. I gave him dried blood leaking out of one of the implants on his back, and a small set of tools at his side for repairs and maintenance of his mechanical parts. However, all of this came later. In the early stages, the idea was simply a creature with mechanical legs and a head resembling a horse skull.

Modeling

After making a sketch of what I was imagining I began roughing out the form with the excellent polygon modeler Clay (www.rocket3d.com). I changed my mind several times about what direction to take the character in. The last sketch was muscular and heroic. I then started modeling him with more inhuman, dinosaur-like proportions, only to finally settle on slim, distorted proportions. Next I took the model into 3ds max. Max has a wide set of procedural modeling tools that were useful in finishing the model and for building the mechanical elements.

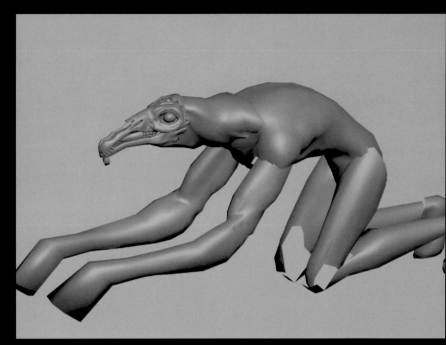

Mechanical reference

Reference for the mechanical parts included photos of a machine gun, motorbike parts, rocket engines and so on. Because the final result was a still image I decided it was more effective to model him directly in the final pose than in a "Da Vinci" generic relaxed pose. My usual approach to modeling is to start with the general form as a low resolution mesh, then go through a process of refining and adding secondary forms and details. I used subdivs for most of the main elements, and used direct/unsubdivided polygon modeling for other parts.

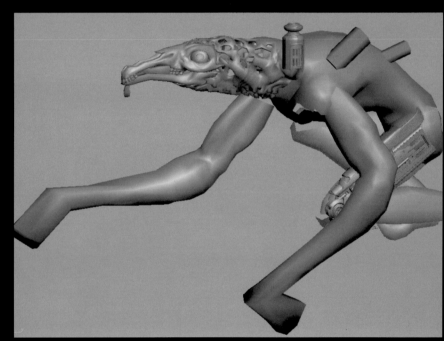

Maximum efficiency

I ultimately split the mesh into several separate objects (arms, torso, head) to make the scene more manageable; straps and belts were useful in hiding the resulting seams. I hate spending forever unwrapping UV coordinates by hand, so I mostly used automatically generated UV coordinates. The only disadvantage of automatic UVs is that they result in a lot of seams. I must admit that I did end up with a few artifacts as a result, but they don't bother me too much and could have been corrected if I had more spare time and motivation.

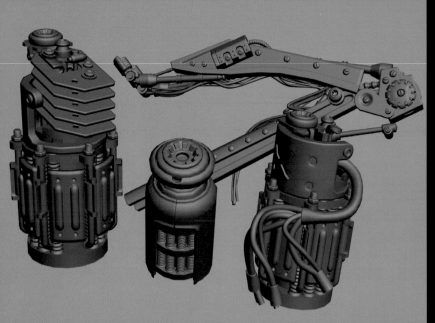

Bevelled edges

I used a Blur Studios script called "wire jumble" to make random paths for all the wires and tubing in the mechanical elements. I made the sharply bevelled edges on the mechanical elements by using a three-edge or "solid" bevel. This is like a normal bevel, but keeps the original edge. In 3ds max try using extrude on an edge, with height set to zero to get an idea of what I mean by three-edge bevel. However it is achieved, a three-edge bevel gives a nice, controllable beveled edge that won't blend off into the surrounding faces.

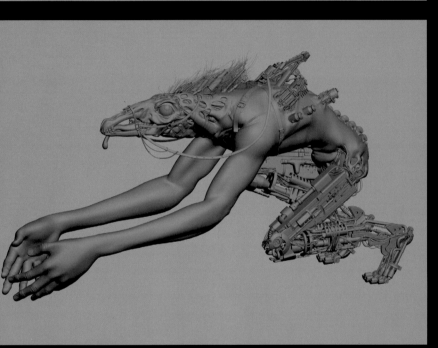

Skin deep realism

I put some specific thought and time into making the areas where mechanical parts join into the flesh. Machinery simply intersecting with the body geometry would look fake and obviously computer-generated, and for that matter wouldn't be much fun. I carefully modeled indentations for each of the mechanical elements to sit into. A lot of the skin has a damaged and torn "swiss cheese" effect in the geometry, I achieved this by using the Cut tool to define the holes and deleting the geometry inside the holes. I used the Relax modifier to make the holes look stretched by the tension of the skin, and I used Solidify ("Shell" in 3ds max 7) to give the holes thickness.

Fine details

For the final stage of detailing I brought some parts of the mesh into ZBrush. With Projection Master I was able to quickly add extremely fine details, which I exported as displacement maps. The hair started out using the plug-in Shag Hair, which I then converted to renderable splines which I edited by hand. I made arm hairs from very simple cylindrical objects, scattered hundreds of times over the surface of the arms using a plug-in called Scatter by Peter Watje.

Texturing

My approach to texturing was to use a lot of procedurals and tiled maps. Knowing that the final result was to be a print resolution image I didn't want to paint texture maps by hand. Texture maps with sufficient resolution would take forever to paint and would eat up huge amounts of memory. Specific details such as redness around the elbows and knuckles came from vertex colors. The base skin map is an image of my forearm scanned on a flatbed scanner (be careful if you do this yourself, the oils in your skin make smudges on your scanner).

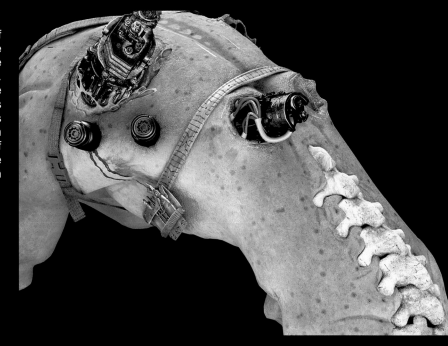

Lighting maps

I gave all the materials a subtle grunge in the crevices by baking out the lighting from a skylight as a map. I then mixed these lighting maps with noise, and turned up the contrast using the map output parameters, and used this to mix grungy colors into my materials. This gives the skin the appearance of dirt and sweat in the wrinkles, and the metal a calcified buildup in the crevices (3ds max 7 users can get the same effect by using the Mental Ray occlusion map). I mixed many layers into the skin material, such as procedural freckles and tan that show up on all the upwards facing surfaces, as well as veins and smudges of mud. I used VRay to render, so I was able to give the materials glossy (blurry) reflections. The result is comparable to specular, but a great deal more realistic.

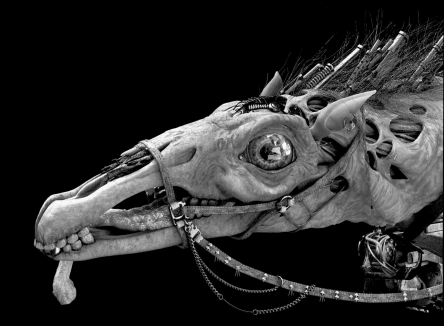

Background

The distant background was made from very simple scattered geometry representing trees (cylinders for trunks, and boxy objects for canopy), and high contrast environment maps—all rendered out of focus. I put several overbright self-illuminated objects behind the trees, which turn into nice soft disks when rendered out of focus (an effect known as Bokeh). One thing I've noticed in photography of out of focus points of light is that imperfections and dust on the lens can make these circles imperfect and grainy. So, I intentionally rendered with low aliasing settings. The resulting noise in the background Bokeh actually adds to the image (and saves me hours in rendering time).

grasses. I made a few variations on size, bend, color and so on so that each grass clump looks naturally random.

Junk

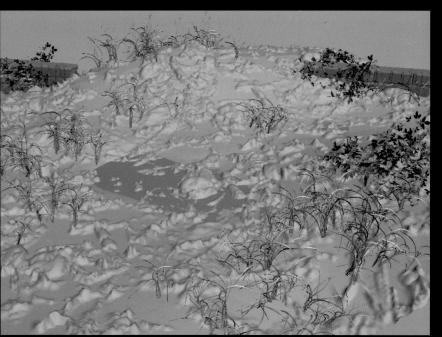

The closer background was a lumpy plane with displacement mapping. The ground was supposed to look like it was composed of junk, like the remains of a really old garbage heap. I made one small square of detailed geometry junk, then from this generated displacement and diffuse maps. By tiling these maps on the ground plane I was able to make it look as though it was made out of hundreds of pieces of garbage, rather than one uniform surface.

Lighting

I lit the scene with area lights, global illumination and a skylight, and used an HDRI map for reflections. I put the strongest lights above and behind the character. I almost always back-light scenes, as it almost always looks better than lighting from the front. By the time I reached the lighting stage I was seriously running out of time; test renders and render passes took a very long time to render, so the final lighting suffers a bit.

Passes

I like to render in passes, which gives me a lot of control to adjust the image in post. The final stage before rendering was setting up some simple rigging for adjusting the pose. The pose and camera placement were a little bit rushed. My intention with both was to take the opposite to normal, expected approach. Normally, one would pose this kind of character in the most dynamic way possible. For better or worse I decided to take the opposite route, so I rendered him in almost perfect profile and in a somewhat static, crouching pose. I had made such a complex character, with so many elements that I ultimately made a few mistakes. Some of the tubing on his back was missing in some passes, so shows up ghostly transparent. A strap is intersecting with the back of his arm, and some ghostly invisible grass can be seen around his hands.

Compromises

Actually rendering the image proved a bit more difficult than I was expecting. When building the materials and textures I didn't bother keeping things as highly optimized as I normally would. Combined with geometry hair, displacement mapping, heavy raytracing and a generally complex scene meant that the use of system resources was excessive, and hitting render resulted in a crash. With only a few days to go (plus full-time work) I had no time to optimize everything, so I replaced some of the displacement mapping with bump mapping, and rendered the hair, legs, head, arms, torso and background separately. A quick test comp of the elements was really disheartening. The image looked awful, and to make matters worse my home computer suddenly stopped working.

Finishing up

I spent the last few evenings after hours at work, desperately making fix-up renders and trying to make the image look good in post using Digital Fusion. I did a great deal of adjusting levels and color grading, darkening and desaturating areas that were too strong, introducing new colors, overlaying gradients and making soft masks. The image was way too chaotic, The figure was lost in the background and the overall colors and lighting were pretty unappealing. I think in the end I dramatically reduced the severity of these problems, though they are still apparent in the final image. I gave the image a slight plumb tint to the shadows, and a blue/green tint to the highlights, and added a slight halo glow around the bright areas, and eventually the image was starting to look much better. I finished off the image with an enormous sense of relief that it turned out to be only a bit of a mess, rather than the utter train wreck mess it could have been. Perhaps the moral is that it's good to plan things out, and not leave things till the last moment.

Ia Soleimani
Runner Up
Machineflesh 3D

Participating in the Challenges has been one of my favorite activities since joining the CGTalk community, and being a part of the 'Machineflesh' was really a great experience for me. It has allowed me to gain new skills in a short period of time, in all areas of CG still imagery. It was my seventh Challenge, so I had to show a major improvement. I had no choice but to make something interesting and more original than the simple ideas that spring to mind when you think of the term 'Machineflesh'. After spending days sketching some ideas for the Machineflesh Challenge I wasn't satisfied with any of my concepts.

I discussed the matter with Fredrick [Eggyt] Wormke about this and came to the conclusion that I should make something comical and in some way related to an animal farm. Fredrick gave me some ideas of his and I joined them with mine to come up with this concept. I showed it to some friends and in the forum. The feedback was good enough to make up my mind. My basic idea behind Machine-cow originally was very dark and more sadistic. For example, I had an idea for using the severed members of the poor cow in another machine for preparing meat products! Eventually, I decided to remove the blood and gore.

The idea

After spending days sketching some ideas for the Machineflesh contest I wasn't satisfied with any of them. I discussed this with Fredrick [Eggyt] Wormke about this and concluded that I should make something comical and related to an animal farm. Fredrick gave me some ideas of his and between us I came up with this concept and showed it to some friends and in the forum. The feedback was good enough to make up my mind.

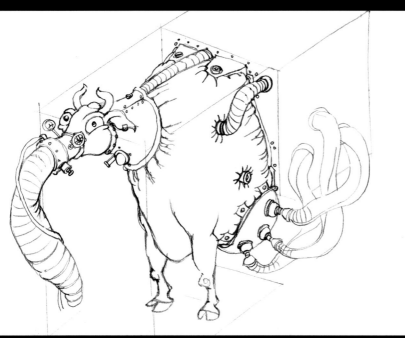

Concept design

My basic idea behind Machine-cow was originally very dark and cruel. For example, I had an idea to use the severed members of the poor cow in another machine for preparing meat products! Later I decided to remove blood and gore. I simplified the idea, but I knew that I'd add some extra things to the image later.

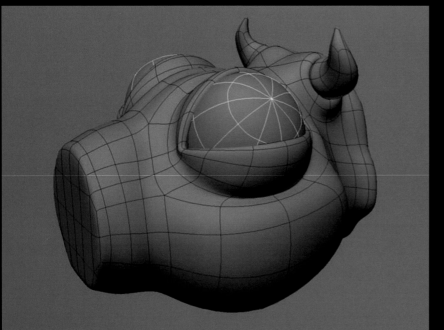

Modeling

For modeling, I used the 3ds max default polygon modeling tools and Loft for pipes.

Modeling order

I started with the Machine-cow head and finished half the body before mirroring it to save effort.

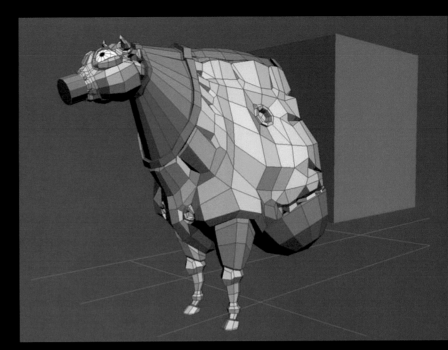

Machine parts

For the machine part, I first placed some blocks for main parts. I then made a series of objects (pipes, connectors, wheels, gears, indicators, etc.) to use like stock parts. I could then easily copy/move them to wherever I needed them, where I'd scale them and deform them. I wanted the machine to look like an early 19th century steam engine.

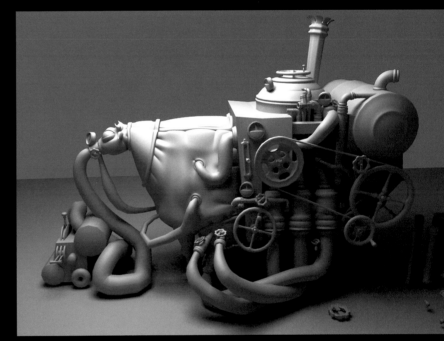

UV unwrapping and texturing

In texturing, I used both procedural and hand-painted bitmaps, and Unwrap and primitive UV mapping. I used mostly procedural shaders for all machine body, parts and pipes. Hand-painted textures with unwrap UV were used for all animals, except the eyes and sheep furs which were all procedurals. I used Photoshop and the 3ds max default unwrapping tool in this stage. Reflections were used for bottles and some machine parts. Andres [Frinsklen] Lazaro was a very good visual advisor here.

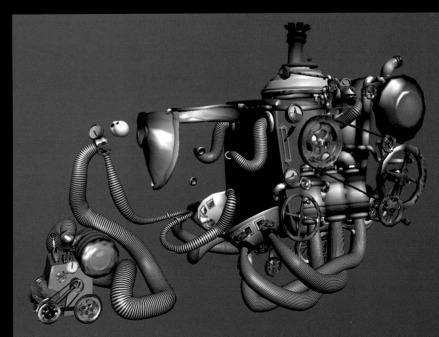

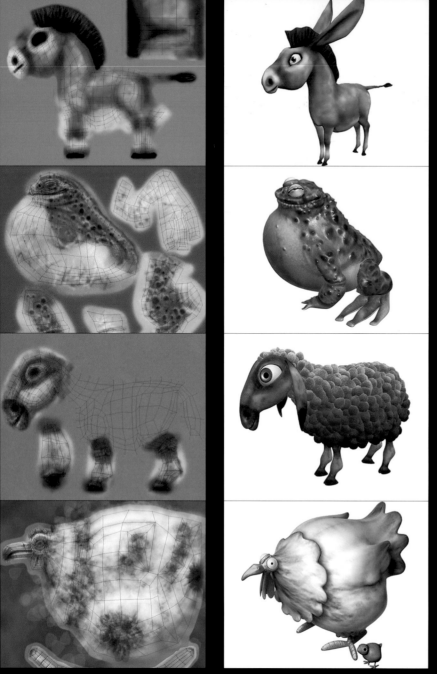

Layout and extra stuff

Later when I was sketching the final composition I decided to add some animals (farm inhabitants) to put in the final image. I wanted them to add some fun and humor, but I was not sure how I could place them and keep the focus on Machine-cow. My solution was to make six animals though I used only three of them of them in the end. At this stage Anders [fellah] Ehrenborg gave me some very useful suggestions to make things better.

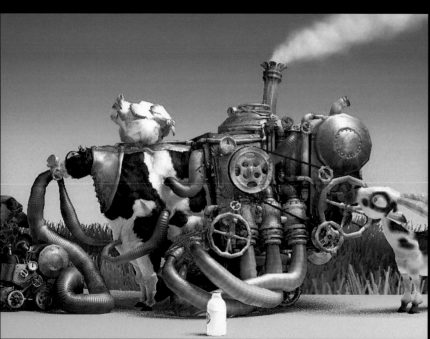

Lighting

Lighting is always my favorite part of creating 3D artwork. There were only two light sources used plus a skylight. I used a 45 degree warm area light for simulating the sunlight and an additional cold tone projecting backlight. VRay was used for rendering with GI turned on. There were no caustic or SSS shaders used.

Composition and color correction

For compositing, layers were rendered separately in 4k resolution, 16bit/channel format (background grass, smoke, vapor, main subject, trees, fences, and foreground grass) and put together in Photoshop. Later I removed the trees. The background sky was painted. I used a Z-depth buffer mask for color-levelling the main subjects. Almost every layer had its own color curve/level adjustment with one adjustment layer applied over the whole image. Hand painting touch-ups were necessary for some parts (e.g. chicken's splotch!).

The final result

David [dobemunk] Maas's advice was very helpful for me to come up with the final composition. I want to thank CGNetworks/CGTalk staff, users, participating partners and kind friends for their gentle thoughts and never-ending support.

Bernardo Delgado

Runner Up

Machineflesh 3D

I've always been drawn to the CGTalk web site as a great source of art from the CG community. To be honest, I was always too afraid to post any of my work because of the really high level of the users. Then a friend (Bernardo Arroyo) entered the Alienware challenge and I thought, why don't I enter a challenge? The CGTalk Challenges also offer artists the opportunity to practice with the support of 3D experts. The Machineflesh challenge was the ideal topic so first I had to decide what to do. I guessed that the entries would be skewed towards monsters and suffering persons so I decided to do something different to make my image unique. The idea I decided to do was an athlete of the future. My mom was the coach of the state track and field team, so I've always admired that sport. I began to imagine the future of robotics and prostheses so I thought it would be nice to make a mix of an athlete and robotic parts to improve his performance. I wanted the picture to be visually interesting so I concentrated on the pose and the backdrop of an aerodynamic testing environment.

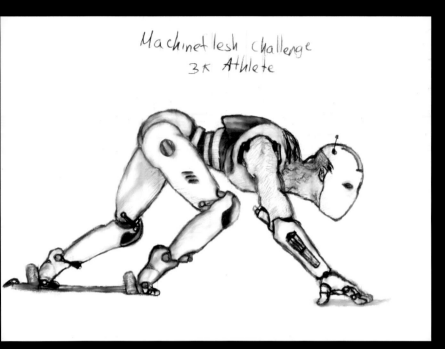

Sketching

Sketching is sometimes one of the hardest steps because it's where you have to express your idea. I made the sketch in a school notebook. I wanted to create a very high-tech athlete but with basic elements to make his functionality look more comprehensive.

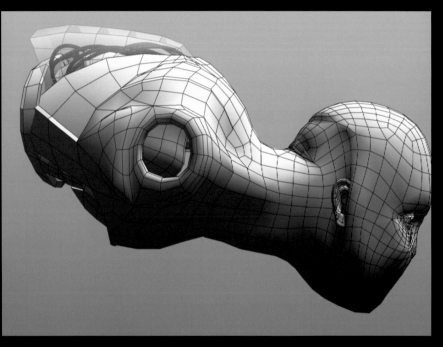

Base modeling

I first made the whole model with basic stuff to guide me, then added more detail. I started with the torso, placing the picture of the sketch into the texture channel to use as a guide for modeling. I started the torso with a simple box and started to give it shape. I used Silo to model this because I personally find it faster to model in. I then exported the torso to 3ds max for the next steps.

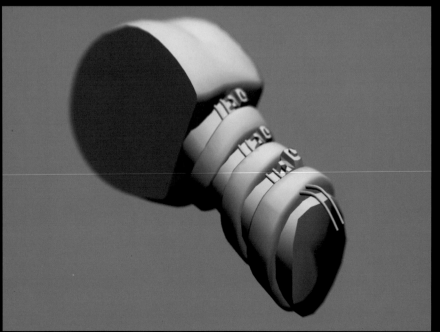

Modeling the hip and butt

From my point of view the hip had to be thin so it could be more aerodynamic, but strong and flexible too. I decided to make it with some kind of metal rings with metal bones at the column to make the function similar to human bones. The inner part of the hip was made of plastic to give it the flexibility it needs to achieve a wider range of movements. The butt was simple to make; I drew a spline in a side view and extruded it with four middle segments. Then I gave it the shape it needed and used the Symmetry modifier.

Legs

The leg's appearance was crucial for this picture because it is one of the most important parts of the athlete model. It has to express strength, but of course it also has to be visually interesting. I decided to make "windows" in the muscle part, so the bloody human muscles would be visible and make the whole concept more human. The leg features sponsor banners for the spectator's benefit and contains impact-absorber material at each join of the parts. The feet had to be able to "open" so I made the feet base separate into two parts, unified by plastic so the feet would be able to flex in the starting position of the athlete.

Arms

Trying to use as much as flesh as possible, I decided to make the arm half-human and half-mechanical. Again, the mechanical part has a "window" in the central part of the impact absorber just to make it more visually interesting. I also decided to change the position of the right arm, because I wanted the character to seem more prepared, powerful and open to the spectator.

Hands

I think hands are always hard to do. I made them really basic—just simple box and sphere modeling. I added some mechanical parts at the base of the hand with the coolest part being the speed indicator on the right hand.

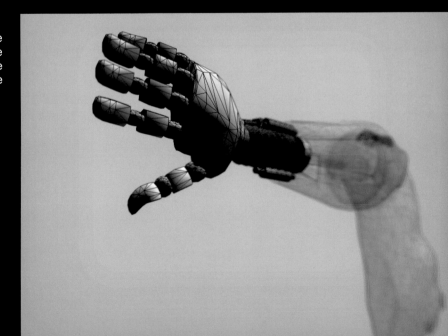

Muscles

Muscles were easy to do using a simple box modeling technique and the MeshSmooth modifier to make them look smooth. The crucial part of the muscles was the texture as it's what convinces the viewer that they are looking at flesh.

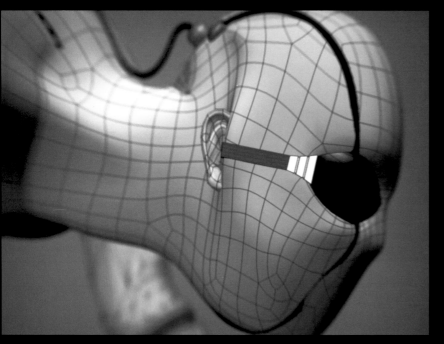

Head

After finishing the "basic" modeling I started to add detail to the face. I thought it would be more appropriate that the face looked human, using a special mask that could be removed after the competition. The mask is made of a special material that reduces air friction and has special glasses to reduce incandescence of the stadium's flares and displays vital information to the athlete.

Track

My first thought was to make the stadium the background, but I didn't think it would improve the composition. I decided to go with a "wind tunnel" aerodynamic testing style. I made a really simple track (that was a single plane) and the models of the feet as impulsors. The most important challenge of the track was to achieve the right effect of a plastic, bumpy surface.

Back

I wanted the character's back to look like the source of the athlete's power. All the most important mechanisms of the character are located there besides the battery. A cable charger plugs into his back and can be disconnected at the precise moment that the athlete starts running.

Shaders

The shaders are essential for the picture, as it gives the objects the ability to express what they are made of. I used car paint shaders for the metallic parts like the legs and arms. I used chrome shaders for the hip metals, while the other objects have simple shaders with just some tweaks.

Texturing

I used Adobe Photoshop, Macromedia Flash and Right Hemisphere Deep Paint to make the textures. I used simple unwraps with the Pack UVs tool to open the objects and create the textures.

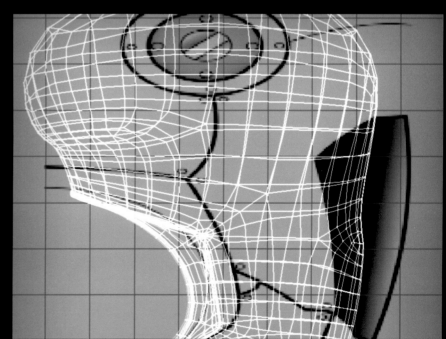

Bernardo Delgado Athlete

Camera

The camera angle was essential for the picture expression. I tried some different angles but was convinced that the most appropriate angle would be a perspective view from the side of the athlete. This angle would show off more of the character.

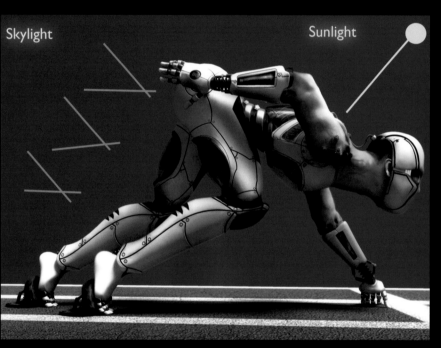

Skylight

Sunlight

Lighting

Lighting gives the picture the artistic feeling. I wanted to use a studio-like lighting setup. I thought it would be cool to create a picture that expresses power and style like a poster of a sports car, so I decided to illuminate the character from the front. I also wanted the picture to look warm and colorful to attract the viewer.

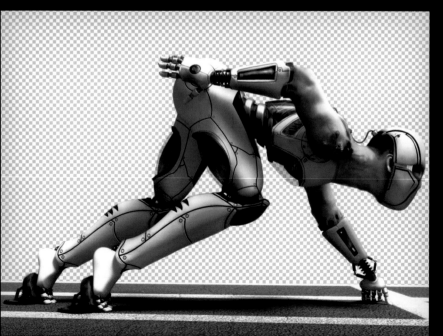

Render

For the rendering I used FinalRender's engine with simple GI and low HDR lighting. I lowered the Raytrace global samples and GI samples to 1/8. And used 16/4 antialiasing samples. I rendered the picture without a background and then created the background in Photoshop.

Composition

Now this was important—the colors I would use to call the eye's attention. As I already had the colors from the track and the character, I thought it would be nicer to use a deep blue background to give it the sport-like appearance. It would create a nice contrast in the picture. I added lots of details like sponsor logos, details to the feet, and the power charger cable in the character's back.

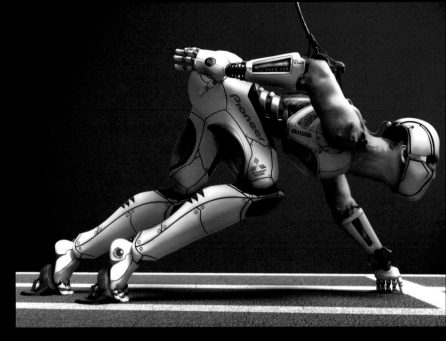

Post effects

I used simple post-effects—especially the diffuse glow. I then drew some "smoke" lines around the character, like in the aerodynamic tests at laboratories. I used smudges to make it look more like smoke and fluid.

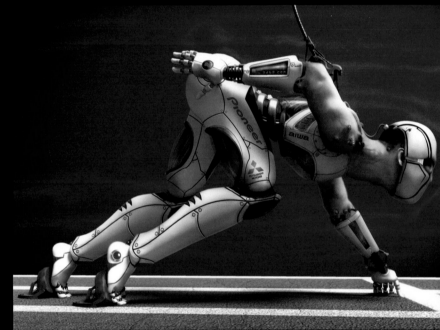

Final

The final result was a picture whose "look and feel" I was satisfied with. I feel that it captured the qualities of the power of the athlete while still having visual appeal. I'd like to thank the CGTalk members for their feedback and I'd like to give special thanks to my friends Mata and Tenorio for their feedback throughout my career.

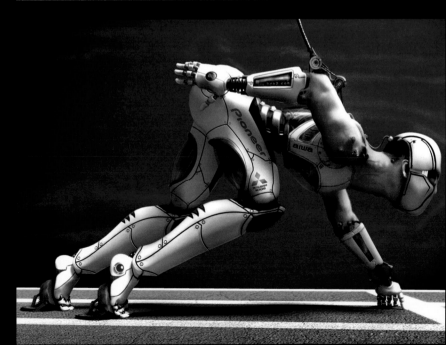

Daryl Mandryk

Winner

Machineflesh 2D

currently work as a character concept
artist at Electronic Arts Canada, where
I've been for over three years. I just
finished up on Def Jam Fight for New
York, and am now working on several
upcoming games. Before my days at
EA, I worked in TV production doing
modeling and texturing. Before that I was
an art student here in Vancouver and way
before that, I was a business student at
university. It's been a long, strange road
but I've basically always been obsessed
with illustrating characters (and art in
general), whether it's 2D or 3D. When
I'm not hunkered down in front of the
computer I like to watch films, play
basketball, draw, and exercise a healthy
videogame addiction. Or sleep.....sleep
is good too. Machineflesh is definitely an
open-ended concept, so I thought the
trick here was to try and do something
different from the majority of the
competition. The one thing I wanted to
avoid, more than anything else, was the
idea of a beautiful girl with wires coming
out of her head. I wanted to get as far
away from that idea as I could, and
also try to avoid spelling out some sort
of deep social commentary. Basically
I wanted to create an image that was,
above all, fun to look at, and secondly, fit
within the guidelines for the contest

A start

When I don't have much of an idea of what I want to paint, I sometimes like to start in black and white. This makes it very easy to just lay down big broad shapes, mess around with them and wait for something to appear. Since I knew that I wanted action and conflict, it had to be two characters, but that was about it. I try to work very rapidly at this point, trying out lots of variations. When I start to focus in on something I like, I'll go in and refine it just a bit. No real details, just a few strokes here and there to describe things. I think this stage took about 30 minutes altogether, and in the end I had my basic concept down—a crazed machine-flesh beast attacking a guy with a gun. You can't get much more basic than that, but often it's the most basic ideas that resonate the most.

Refinement and color

Since I didn't really follow the traditional 2D workflow laid out by the contest, my lineart milestone was more of a tightening and refining of my initial sketch. At this point I tried to add some medium details to the image, and make some big decisions regarding the composition and layout. This is where working digital is great, as you can easily cut out, scale, rotate, or otherwise transform elements of the picture until it looks right to your eye. Black and white is fine for blocking something out quickly, but if the final product is a painting, you really need to start adding and working with color quickly. I knew I wanted to avoid painting the entire image in grayscale then colorizing it, as this doesn't look good at all. You'll end up with something that looks like a colorized black and white film—it just looks wrong, and can take a long time to fix. So after I had a rough black and white, I immediately put a color wash over the top of the whole thing using a multiply layer. This acts almost like an under painting. and allows you to go over the top of it with colors, sculpting out forms and tightening shapes up.

Capturing the essence

This is where things start to get fun. This screenshot represents around 3-4 hours of work, just blocking in big shapes and colors. All of the original black and white image has been painted over, but that's ok since it was basically just a template for the final painting. A lot of the drawing is off, but I'm not really too worried about it at this point. I'm shooting for mood and overall idea here, just trying to capture the essence of what the painting is all about and answer all the basic questions. Anatomy is warped, and everything looks very rough, but all that will be tightened up later. I'm also working at a pretty low resolution since all the details will come later. Since I work in Painter, it also allows me to work more quickly since my PC sometimes has trouble keeping up with high resolution brush strokes. I'm also starting to think about a background at this point. The temporary scrapyard idea was just way too boring. I'm a big fan of loose, nebulous backgrounds, which probably stems from my dislike of painting architecture. The trick is you still need to put in enough detail to keep it interesting, and at this point I wasn't sure what to do—I just threw a bit of color down and waited for something to appear. Experimentation is key here. One technique I learned from those Ryan Church DVDs is to copy your image to a new layer, mess around with it, and then erase out areas you don't want. This is a great way to try lots of variations until something strikes you.

Sculpted

Here I start to tighten things up more. Notice especially on the hero character, the details of his suit are starting to come through. What was once just a rough block-in of a bit of value and color are now beginning to be sculpted out into something that looks much more 3D. I start the same process on the monster, spending some time on the face and arm figuring out just how the machinery and skin interact. I start to work on the idea that the monster has received a wound from the hero's weapon. It gives a bit of backstory and reason why this beast looks so pissed off.

Uprez and glow effects

It's finally time to uprez and really begin tightening up the painting. I uprez the image to about 2,600 x 4,100 pixels, 300dpi. This will allow me to put in a good amount of detail without bogging down my computer too much. I went in with the Glow brush of Painter 7 and added lots of nice glow effects on the lava, as well as some fire streaming from the monster's arm. I remember feeling that things were really starting to fall into place at this point—the warm glows really gave the painting a lot more energy. Again, more detail starts to show through as I tighten up edges and get even more specific.

Realistic details

I try to work in some more realistic details such as sparks and blood spatters. There were several hot spots in the previous version that were just reading to white—the hero's arm in particular. I try to help it out by putting a slight shadow map layer over the offending areas. The metal which was reading as grey plastic before is looking better. I'll still have to go in and give it some specular highlights, but that comes later.

The home stretch

I briefly toy with the idea of leaving it flipped like this, but in the end decide it doesn't quite read as well. Still—it reads almost as well, and that's a good sign that composition is working pretty good. I've added a load of details here, and things in general are feeling a lot more solid. I start to play around with colors a bit here and there—you'll notice the rocks have a lot more green in them. The blue of the hero's suit helps set him apart from his adversary, and complements his weapon. I spent a good deal of time on the lava as well, just adding bits and pieces flying around—really trying to drive home the action, and sell the flow of the piece. I want the background to serve the painting, helping the viewer's eye move around as much as possible, then coming to rest on the focal points. I consider leaving it at this point and calling it finished, but a few things are still bugging me.

The final image

This is where I really go for the knockout punch and pull out all the stops. I make countless small adjustments and put the final polish on the characters. Near the end of the painting, I decide the large 'horns' on the monster's elbows aren't working. I spend some time reworking it a bit, into several smaller pointy bits of metal. It's a small change, but it helps a lot in the balance of the monster design. The greenish rocks also had to go, and I went with something much more like lava-rock—dull flat black. Final FX are put in, such as the glowing blue residue on the monster's wound. My goal is to have enough detail that the viewer whole-heartedly buys into the painting, but not so much detail that they are overwhelmed by it, and the painting feels static. When I feel as if I've struck this balance, I know it's time to stop. All the great feedback I received really helped a lot in pulling this image together. Thanks to all who contributed with critiques and suggestions, they really helped. See you all in the next challenge!

Jeff Rey

Runner Up

Machineflesh 2D

I've been drawing since I was a small child and dreamed of going to art school. Unfortunately, art school didn't want me, so I followed the path of the self-taught artist. I've illustrated many childrens' books, along with commercial illustration work. For the last ten years I've worked in the games industry including work in concept art and game illustrations. I'm currently working on my own project, a comic book of which I've also completed the script—truly satisfying work. For the Machineflesh Challenge, I found the theme very inspiring. Obviously, it was going to feature a lot of warlike machine entries, so I wanted to find an idea a little bit different— maybe in opposition to the war theme. I launched into my entry with the idea of machines of peace. My initial concept lacked power, so I chose a more dynamic character whose role was to act as a demonic animal guardian.

A start

I have the beginnings of an idea of what I want to paint. I sketch a lot, trying to find the precise idea. I sometimes like to start in black and white, laying down shapes, then mess around with them until I find the direction I want to go. For this Challenge, I knew that I wanted a very natural integration of machine and flesh. I work slowly at this point, trying to find an intuitive result. I finally decide that this concept is not effective enough for the Challenge. I need something more powerful, and stranger. Thinking more about the integration of machinery and flesh I came up with a machine-head. This would imply a kind of rejection of the body, with the degeneration of flesh as a consequence. I used myself as model, and started to work using a tablet and Painter.

Finally, a direction

At the machine-level I include heaps of valves, pipes, and mechanisms mixing with the biological being. I explored the concept of a warrior—not with super plasma guns, but with a mega-muscular and rather demonic body at the center. The back story began to develop in my mind: the character is an empty carcass animated by one violent spirit—a puppet-body, without control of himself, except the rage and madness. He is a demon with little devil imps controlling (and injuring) his machineflesh body—almost like pilots for individual limbs.

A second start, a real start

I often start work on the values, then add the shade and light for each part. I work on the details looking to see what develops. Usually we're taught to paint with a global eye, which is a good priciple, but it's also a point of view. I often work on the details to start with right across the piece. Sometimes I'll use photo reference and study details for a long time—how the light is affecting objects depending on their material—and then I'll start to paint. When I have done one type of element I know how it works and I leave the photo reference behind. I'll paint other objects with the example in mind, allowing surprises to occur. I don't like to control everything. I like to give chance a chance. At this stage I'm working at a high resolution, to accommodate the details. I prefer to work with Painter's very basic brushes. I'm also starting to think about a background at this point. The temporary idea is to draw a fly-scape of a human city.

Let's play

I begin the real detail work. As my character is a demon, his weapons needed to inspire a mood of death, so I settle on skulls. I choose animal skulls because the character is the avatar-guard of the wildlife of the forest. For setting colors I work with Photoshop. I have a layer for each element—approximately 30 layers for this piece. I prefer to use live models, but sometimes it's difficult to have everything available when it's needed. As the detail work advances, I merge the layers into more coherent Layer sets. This gives me the freedom to work on the background, or other elements at once.

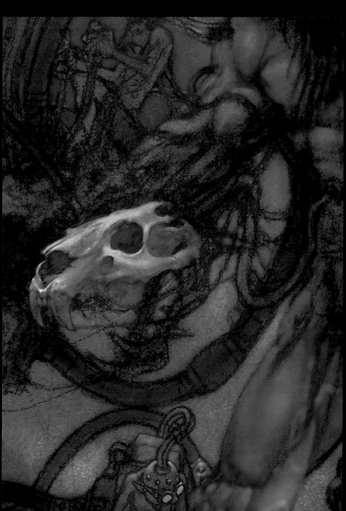

I upsize the image resolution to allow me to work very deeply in the image. The file is now about 3,040 x 4,000 pixels, at 300dpi. I test different effects using Photoshop's blending modes. I'll often use the Multiply blend mode to give me new ideas as I work, but I tend to try all blend modes layer-by-layer. To test the piece, I often completely desaturate it. This gives me the ability to see whether the values stay correct. I also play with zoom, reducing picture on screen to a stamp scale. This is a good way to find mistakes, and is a little like painting on a traditional canvas and getting some distance from it. I focus on the main body and all the details inside of which there are a lot. The background has changed again, though I'll leave it for the moment. I work with a very basic brush in Photoshop—no size effect, and an opacity of about 11% or sometimes even as low as 5%. I start with a big brush and then work down in size. Most of the elements are still very rough—especially the little imps.

More details

The background finally appears. I try to give it a perspective to focus on the center of the body. To enhance the balance of the character I draw a little path behind him, all in curves, with a start point at his right foot. I create a new layer that I fill with one color that allows me to focus on the next phase—defining the values. Most of the work is done, except the frontier between background and foreground elements—a question of lighting. It's time to work on the lights and the shadows. This is where working digital is so great. I create a shadow layer and a light layer, playing with blending modes and contrast. The background also allows me the ability to detach a lot of parts of the figure. I always play with the "Opposition" principle. For me it's a basic law: shadow-light, hard-soft, nebulous-precise, etc.

Harmonization

It's time to play again with blending options and the colors—not a huge amount, but just to get an indication of what is working. I create some layers and play with blending modes to see the color interactions. I work here with a big basic brush, and different opacities depending on the blending options. I now start to harmonize the background and figure and continue to work on the details—the little imps are almost done.

The final image

I tidy up the last of the details on the demon's piping. I add some shadows and specular effects, especially toward the bottom of the legs. Harmonization with the background is complete, so I can focus now on the global color balance. I gained a lot of pleasure participating in this Challenge. I met great people and maybe future friends. It was really very interesting to work with others on the same theme, looking at everyone's take on the same theme. It was very inspiring. Thanks to CGTalk, CGNetworks and Ballistic Publishing for this great idea and for their hard work.

Damian Bajowski

Runner Up

Machineflesh 2D

'm 24 years old and live in Bialystok city
n Poland where I study architecture at
a local university. Besides becoming an
architect I mess with my friends from the
Evermotion team (www.evermotion.org)
where I'm responsible for textures and
all 2D-related stuff. Currently, I'm trying
to familiarize myself with 3D software
because I find it fascinating the level of
quality you can create. The main idea
of my Machineflesh entry was to create
something funny rather than totally scary
and dark. I didn't want someone to
look at my entry as something in bad
taste. Instead of creating some vicious
machinery with flesh stuck here and
here, I tried to make something closer
to a cartoon feel. I thought some kind of
dog would be great. My first inspiration
was the famous Looney Tunes' "Spike"
character. The second inspiration was
the dog that belongs to Lobo, the comic
character. I remember reading one of
Lobo's adventures illustrated by Simon
Bisley a couple of years ago and the
design of the dog character was just
great. It was scary and funny at the
same time, and that was the goal of my
Machineflesh Challenge entry—to create
something like that.

Damian Bajowski Puppy

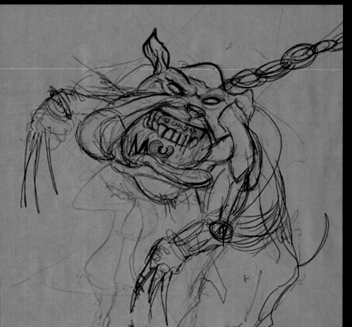

Sketch

Since I'm used to drawing from scratch using color I didn't put much effort into this first step. I caught the nearest pencil and in a few minutes made a sketch just to get the right composition. It was very unimpressive stuff, but I did it just to complete the required milestone. I already had the base idea of what mechanical parts my "puppy" should have but I didn't think it was useful including them at this stage. I didn't want all those hi-tech blinking gadgets that can be seen in most sci-fi movies. I wanted implants made of rusty junkyard garbage instead—a mix of a car wreck and a dog. I thought it would be much more original than another future-designed android.

Coloring

I started with dark tones in Painter using its various brushes—mostly the "Palette Knife" and some from the "Oils" and "Pastels" categories. Basically, these are my favorites. What I really like about Painter is how you can easily make a mess with all those tools simulating natural media. That's why it's just perfect to start with and design a whole image. I knew I didn't want my picture full of various colors but rather dominated by one color scheme. That's why I used mostly bronze in the beginning. When the image was dirty enough, I decided to let some light in and increase contrast by putting some dark spots here and there. Now it was ready to start the real work. I tried to create the right color scheme and range and mark most of the details but without finishing them—just to have the base idea of the final result.

Color experimentation

I think the most creative and interesting part of the process is where you can notice and realize how various colors put in the same place creates totally different effects and can bring your work to a higher level. I spent a couple of hours doing my best to get as good a result as possible conducting experiments with colors and brushes. I don't know why, but I pierced doggy while messing with its tongue. It was one of those ideas which hits your mind suddenly, and you find it extremely cool. I also drew two big screws stuck to the doggy's back. Finally, I found it finished enough to switch to Photoshop and start working on the details.

nto Photoshop

don't like doing detail work in Painter. I think
just got used to Photoshop's brush control and
ow it works with pressure-sensitive hardware.
started from color adjustment and turned the
vhole color scheme into red. I tried with different
olors but the red seemed to be best. I did it
ecause I realized I had got too far away from my
orimary idea of keeping the image in one color
ange. After that I drew a little kitty—very flat
vithout deep shading so that it couldn't be seen
t first look.

Refinements

The next step was to get more contrast. I added
ighter parts on the dog with a low opacity brush.
wanted to give it more space, especially between
he dog's face and razor arm in the background.
There's no doubt that the face should dominate
here, so I tried to bring it forward. With a small-
sized brush, I put very bright highlights on the fur
o give an extra strong light source effect. I then
moved on from the foreground to start working on
he environment. It's fortunate that I added some
valls. At first, I wanted to leave the image with an
unfinished look, but then it looked too undefined.
made some holes in the wall caused by machine
claws and added a plastic bowl with "Spike" on
t. A couple of mixed dirt maps overlaid at low
ayer opacity got rid off the wall's smoothness. I'm
not sure to this day if it was a good step. Finally,
decided to leave it. It made the whole image
ook darker.

Final

didn't want to make the whole image over-
detailed so I left most of the background
untouched. I just added some little stones at the
oottom. Overall this was one of those images
hat you really enjoy moving forward. Everything
went according to plan, and I managed to finish
t in about 12 hours total. I want to thank all the
people who voted on this one and made me 2nd
runner up. It gives me great motivation and belief
n my capabilities. Thanks!

Francis Tsai

Runner Up

Machineflesh 2D

I was excited to read about an art competition based on the theme of combining flesh and machine. The "Machineflesh" term itself provided a great "seed" for the visual development process. My initial word-association reflex resulted in the sort of post-Terminator, cyborg-type imagery one might expect. After some further consideration I felt this topic could provide a good opportunity to work against those sorts of expectations, and create a character design that I wouldn't normally do. One of my primary visual influences is actually a writer named H.P Lovecraft—particularly his short stories about "Ancient Ones", travelling through time, and "Elder gods". After thinking about "Machineflesh" for a few days, I came up with a simple, heavily Lovecraft-ian back story, which I summarized with the title "Reluctant God". My idea for combining flesh and machine centered around a fictitious 19th century academic researcher (Bernard) whose efforts would result in his being fused with his machinery. His research project involved travelling through time, and designing a machine to help him achieve that goal. In this story, due to some miscalculation or oversight, Bernard was thrust into the distant future, much further than he had intended, to a time when humanity had long since disappeared. The Earth was unrecognizable, populated with strange life forms. In addition, Bernard himself was painfully distorted and somehow irreversibly bonded to his machine.

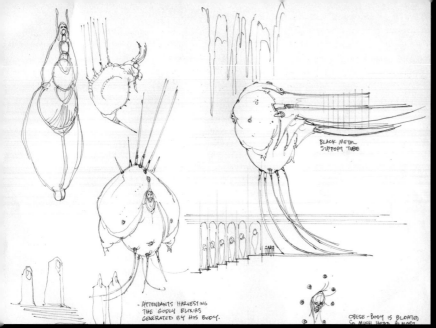

Thumbnail passes

The first thumbnail passes were attempts to significantly alter Bernard's silhouette, to make a creature that was clearly not a normal human being. In these early versions, I had the idea that the bizarre machineflesh creature would be perceived as some sort of god by the people of the distant future, to go along with the concept of "Reluctant God". I also started thinking that it was important that the character's face be clearly visible—I wanted to be able to rely on that to convey a sense of anguish and despair.

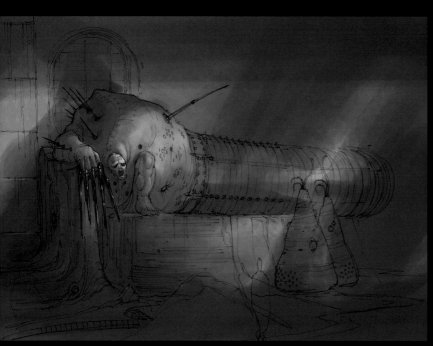

Color sketch

In the color sketch, I tried developing the "fat guy" concept a little more. Here, he is seated on a kind of throne rather than hanging from some sort of apparatus. The earlier sketches of the hanging fat guy design were too reminiscent of the Baron Harkonnen character from Frank Herbert's Dune. I thought pushing the design more in the direction of Lovecraft would help to avoid that comparison, but it still looked very "Dune" to me. At this point I realized I hadn't really investigated the aesthetic design of the "machine" portion of the character to any great extent, and that the Lovecraft angle wasn't giving me enough to work with visually. It seemed like I needed to bring in some other ideas or influences, to help move the character design aspect along.

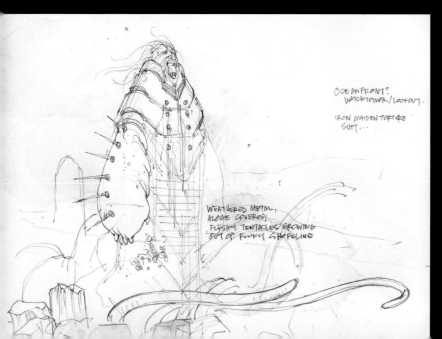

Mythology

There are many instances in mythology where someone is punished for defying the wishes of a higher power. The myths of Prometheus (who brought fire to humanity, and was punished by having his innards torn out repeatedly by an eagle) and Sisyphus (who defied the gods and so was forced to push a heavy stone up a hill, which would then roll back down, causing him to go through the same process endlessly) seemed to be great sources from which to draw inspiration. In this sketch, I tried thinking of Bernard in these terms, as if he were sentenced to some sort of eternal hell or torture for daring to defy the gods and travel through time. In this version, I imagined Bernard as a sort of watchman at the edge of the ocean. Because he is essentially rooted where he stands, his flesh would be subject to the harsh elements, kept alive by his machinery.

Color blocking

I went with that idea, eventually eliminating the ocean in favor of a nondescript hellish landscape. I figured I would come up with something a bit more interesting for the environment later. For now I was still mainly concerned with the character design. Here are a few steps in the color blocking in process, with a slight detour as I tried a female version. I decided pretty quickly that it was too distracting—this project wasn't really about painting attractive female forms, so I went back to the twisted male torso version. During this time, I had also been reading a book called 'Art & Physics' by Leonard Shlain, in which he talks about some of the parallels between various art movements and certain theoretical and practical breakthroughs in classical physics and quantum mechanics. A portion of the book was devoted to time travel (theoretical of course) and how certain art styles might be interpreted as trying to represent that phenomenon visually. One section in the book talked about how as a (travelling) observer approaches the speed of light, the object he is observing will actually become deformed. Quite a mind-bender, especially for someone interested in the nature of perception to begin with. Relativistic theory states that at the speed of light, length (in the direction of travel) can become so compressed that it is possible to see both backward and forward simultaneously. I've tremendously oversimplified the material I read, but some of the concepts discussed in the book provided tremendous visual inspiration. In particular, I was intrigued by the "backwards-forwards" idea, and the idea of something being distorted along its length due to relativistic forces.

Machine elements

At this point in the rough color block-in stage, I still felt as though something was missing, like I hadn't really incorporated the machine element well enough. I took a break from the painting and sketched out some ideas for a time machine aesthetic. Since the end product was to be a 2D painting, I was purely interested in silhouette, rather than in trying to design a believable, functional machine. I also thought it would be nice to hint at some of the concepts from the Shlain book with the shape design of the machine.

Visual vocabulary

With this image, I was finally starting to feel like the painting was getting somewhere. Bernard's head has been forcibly turned 180 degrees from his body, and he has somehow been both fused with and impaled on his time machine device. In addition, the machinery itself seems to be stretched out and distorted along one axis, as a result of its journey through time (with its unexpected relativistic "side effects"). I spent a relatively short time on the thumbnailing exercise for the time machine. The visual vocabulary of long, directional spiky forms which quickly emerged in the thumbnails seemed to be a satisfying visual complement to the amorphous nature of Bernard's body, and so I felt comfortable enough with the basic vocabulary for the time machine aesthetic to go back to the painting.

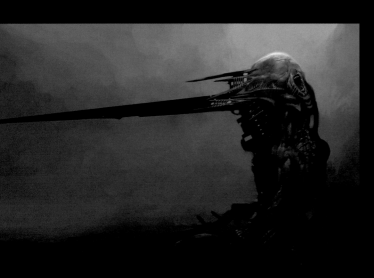

Facial expression

Because I felt as though I had a reasonably solid plan for the painting as a whole, I was able to relax and concentrate on painting the face of the character. I knew that any impact the image had was going to depend heavily on how the emotion was expressed in the facial expression, and that the face would be the focal point of the painting. I was also depending on the long spiky forms of the time machine aesthetic to help me "manage" the composition and reinforce that focal point. I wasn't really happy with the way the eyes and general expression were working in this version. Often in a character-based painting I find that I will paint several versions of a face over the initial block-in, searching for the one that seems to best fit the character and the needs of the piece.

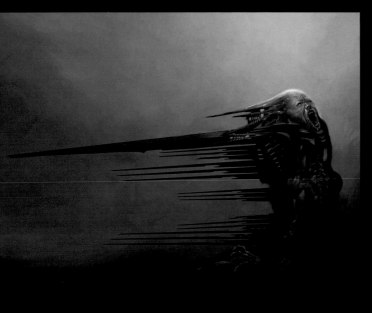

Refining and tweaking

One source of visual inspiration that I had discovered recently was the work of an artist named Zdzislaw Beksinski. His work is similar to H.R. Giger's in that much of it consists of surreal, somewhat abstract and vaguely biomorphic figures and architecture. To me, Beksinski's work often conveys a distinct sense of place, whereas Giger's work seems to be more about textures and sculpture. I love the work of both artists, but for my own painting I drew more inspiration from Beksinski's work. Perhaps because I come from an architectural background, Beksinski's imagery felt more "inhabitable" than Giger's—it was easier to imagine myself inside his paintings. The other aspect of many of Beksinski's paintings that I enjoy is the soft, diffuse lighting. Many of his paintings have a light quality that feels very eerie and dreamlike. It's difficult to tell what time of day it is in some of his paintings, or from what direction it's coming from. I wanted to capture that same sense of eerie, indistinct lighting, and to emulate his ability to create a convincing surreal world.

Moving in the right direction

This image and the previous one show the development of the final face "design", as well as some back and forth on the time machine component. At this point, I was pretty happy with the overall read. The character design and composition of the page seemed to be communicating the ideas I was interested in, and it appeared that the decision to increase the horizontal proportions gave the piece a more dynamic feel.

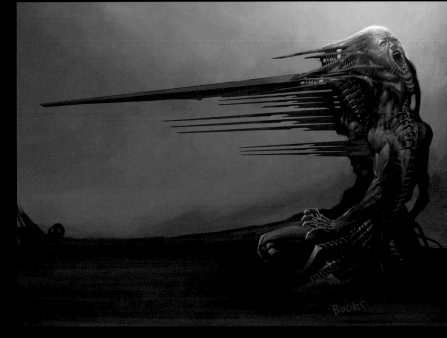

Refining and tweaking

All that remained from this point was refining the painting, tweaking color and values for mood and readability. I let it sit in this state for a few days to let the concept percolate in the back of my mind. When I came back to it, it seemed that there might be another layer I could add to help reinforce the story. I copied and pasted a few versions of the main figure back into the painting, altering each one slightly. The idea was that the multiple versions of Bernard in various incarnations would represent his journey through time (similar to Einstein's "twins" paradox)—his deformation becoming more and more pronounced. The boundary between man and machine getting ever more blurred. In the murky fog in the foreground, I placed the equations for the Lorentz-Fitzgerald contraction, which describes the length-distortion phenomenon I mentioned earlier, as a sort of geeky in-joke. The strange towers were meant to evoke the "god" in the reluctant god concept, as if they were temples erected by some distant-future life forms to pay respects to the tortured Bernard-god.

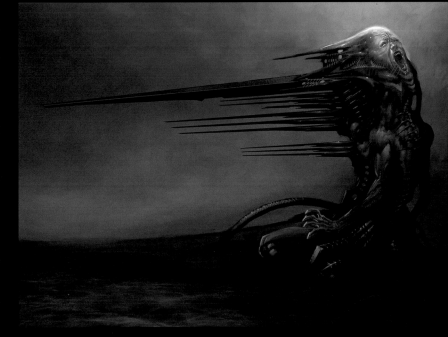

Hindsight

In retrospect, I probably would have devoted a little more time to developing the architecture of the distant future. Some of the Lovecraft time travel short stories devote quite a bit of text in describing the architecture of the distant past/ future, and were a great source of inspiration for me years ago. As with the design of the time travel machinery, I think the trick would have been in coming up with something interesting design-wise for the architecture which would also support the story idea and not distract from the overall emotional read of the character. Another element I had thought about was portraying humanity's descendants in some form. One idea I had was to include a number of small, partly flesh and partly mechanical spider-like creatures scurrying around the base of the main creature. These would of course be the result of millions of years of evolution, and could probably have been another machineflesh project in itself.

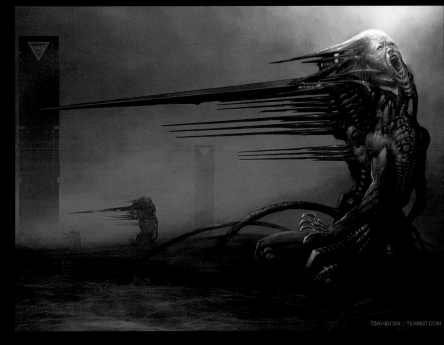

TSAI 061304 :: TEAMGT.COM

The light at the top
3ds max, VRay, Photoshop
Ivelin Yordanov, BULGARIA

Domination
LightWave 3D, Photoshop
Norman Rosenstech, FRANCE

Zoo Girl
Photoshop
Jonny Duddle, UNITED KINGDOM

Tortured Souls
Painter, Photoshop
Jason Chan, USA

Cybernetic Basketball Player
Photoshop
Thierry Bonnet, bOne, FRANCE

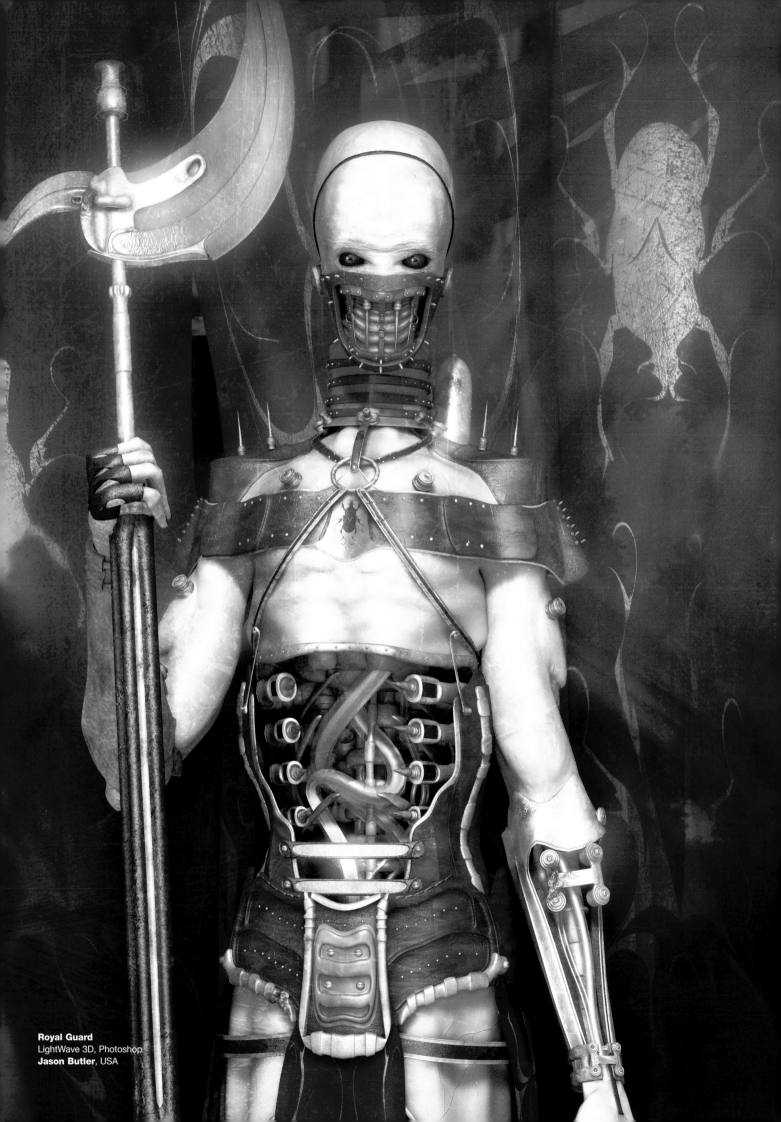

Royal Guard
LightWave 3D, Photoshop
Jason Butler, USA

Kinnaree
Maya, Photoshop, BodyPaint
Udom Ruangpaisitpron, THAILAND
[top]

Ripper
3ds max, Mental Ray, Photoshop
Gary Pate, Sydney, AUSTRALIA
[above]

Steam
Digital Fusion
Yvan Verhoeven, BELGIUM

Slave
Painter, Photoshop
Alex Kaiser, County Cork
IRELAND
[top]

Cybermaid
Painter, Photoshop
Alena Klementeva,
RUSSIAN FEDERATION
[above]

Dancers
Painter
Monsit Jangariyawong,
THAILAND
[above]

Kraken
Traditional/Digital
Paul Davidson,
UNITED KINGDOM

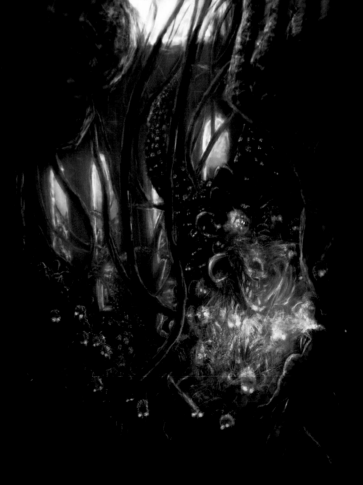

Electrochimere
Photoshop
Friedric Petrequin,
Heavydarkness Studio, FRANCE
[top]

Bee Queen
Photoshop
Pablo Valbuena, SPAIN
[above]

Welcome To The Machine
Photoshop, Painter
Nick Clark, Sinister Flamingo
Productions, CANADA
[above]

Return to the deep
Painter
Brian J. Read,
NEW ZEALAND

Fallos
Photoshop
Frederick Meier, DENMARK

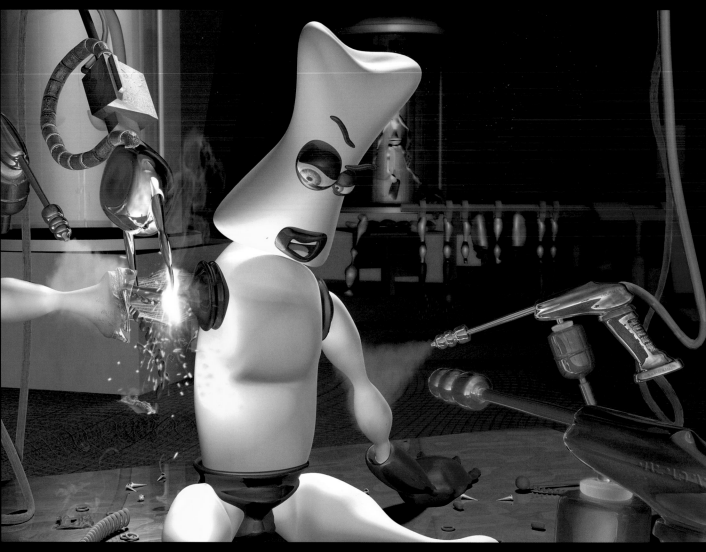

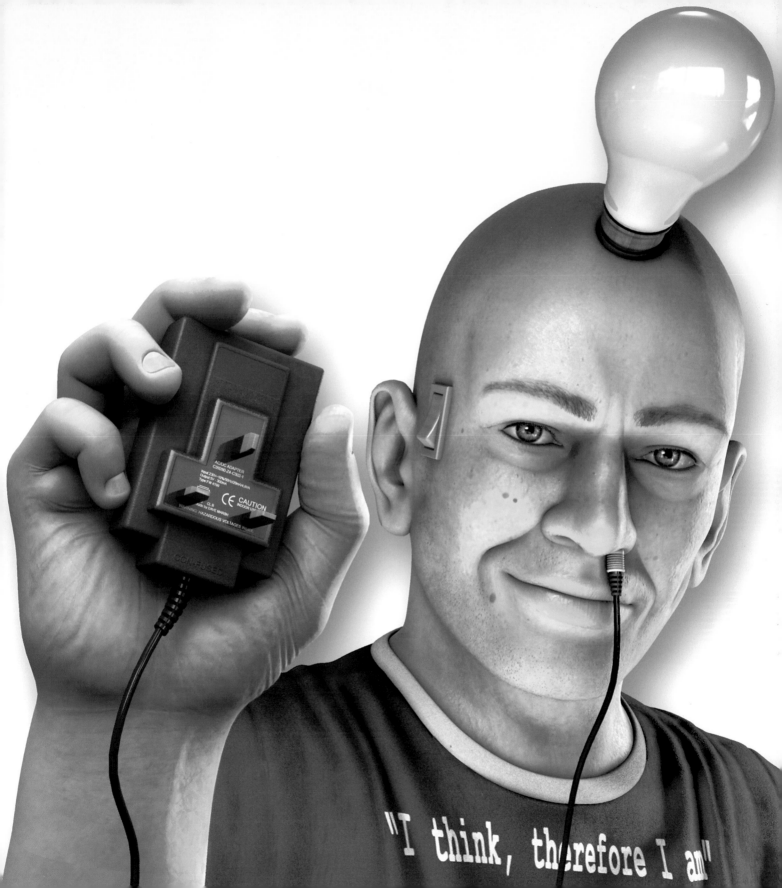

Hunters
Photoshop
Richard Dumont, CANADA
[left]

Learning to Fly
Photoshop
Panu Uomala, FINLAND
[right]

WARNING !
TEST FLIGHTS
WHEN LIGHT ON.
KEEP CLEAR OR
CLOSE TO A
TRAINER !

Sacrament of birth
Painter
Roman Gunyavy, UKR
[left]

Collier of the Future
Painter
Yura Vranchan,
RUSSIAN FEDERATION
[right]

Cyber Dragon
Photoshop
Teemu Rajala, FINLA
[far left]

Mechawaste
3ds max
Andrzej Poturalski, F
[left]

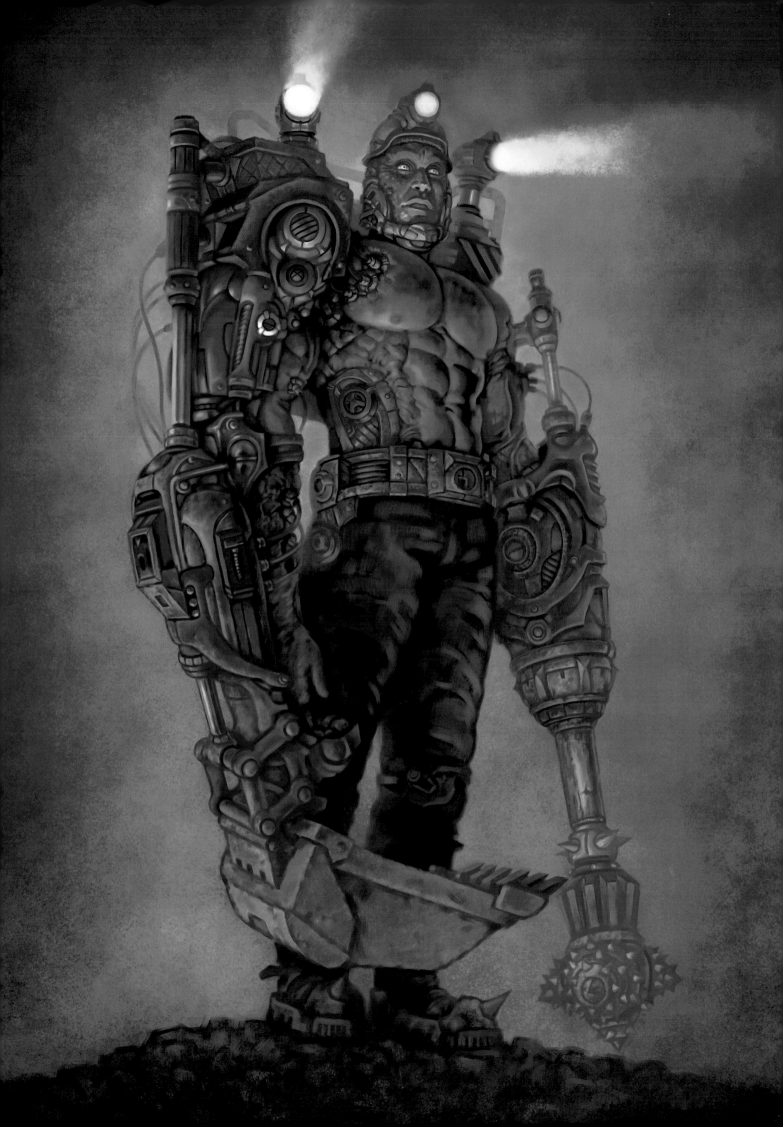

The Butterfly of love
3ds max, VRay
Pavel Fedorchuk,
RUSSIAN FEDERATION

Cyber-Frog
Maya, Photoshop
Kurt Boutilier, CANADA

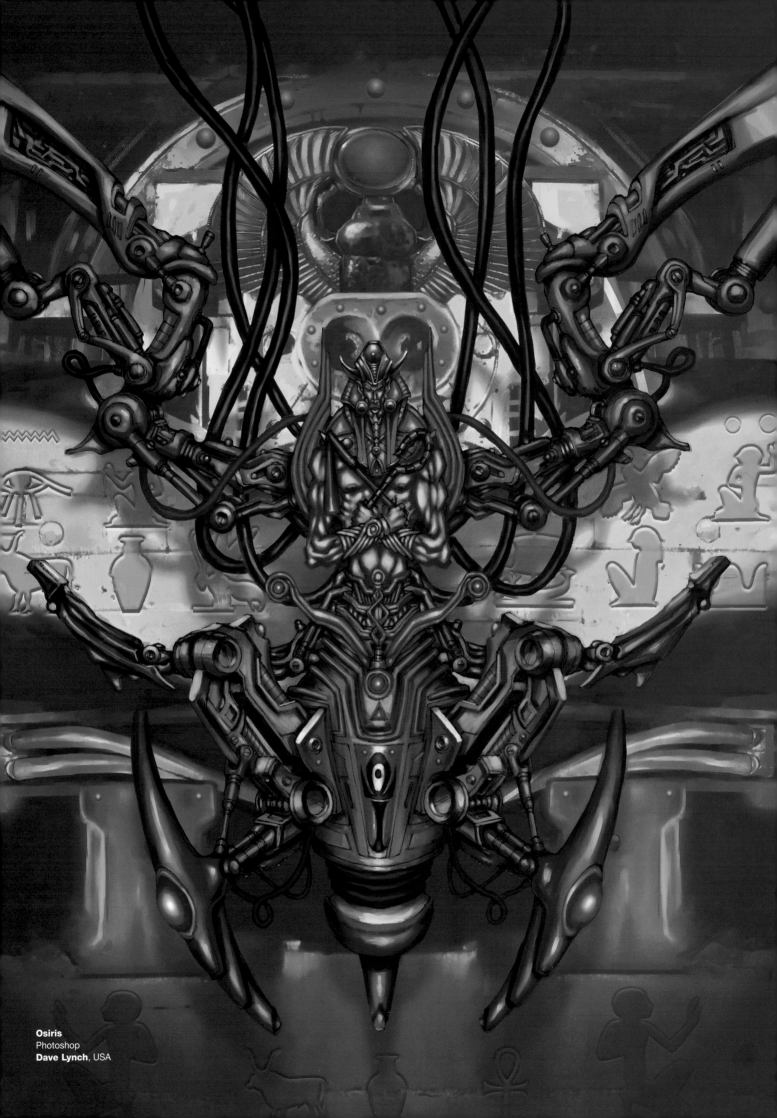

Osiris
Photoshop
Dave Lynch, USA

The New War
mental ray, Photoshop
Jeffrey M. Brown, USA
[top]

Sawhead the lion
flame, Photoshop
Julien BONNET, FRANCE
[above]

A Future of Mechanical Trees
Photoshop
Marek Okon, Toronto CANADA

Index

A

Søren 'Trenox' Andersen
DENMARK
trenox.junkworks.org
86

B

Damian Bajowski
Evermotion
POLAND
www.evermotion.org
50-53

Charles 'Baby' Beirnaert
FRANCE
babystudio@wanadoo.fr
6

Pascal Blanché
UBISOFT
Montreal Quebec CANADA
www.3dluvr.com/pascalb/
6

Julien Bonnet
36 rue Murillo
92170 Vanves
FRANCE
www.kraschtm.fr.st
92

Thierry Bonnet
bOne
47 Avenue du Général
Michel Bizot 75012 Paris
FRANCE
http://bonestudio.free.fr
68, [Back cover: CGChallenge
Machineflesh]

Kurt Boutilier
CANADA
81x.com/akboots/kurtboutilier/
88-89

Jeffrey M. Brown
Aeon Logic
Longmont, Colorado USA
www.opusthirteen.com
92

Jason Butler
Atlanta, USA
flinder@gofalldown.com
71

C

Jason Chan
California, USA
www.jasonchanart.com
65

Matt Clark
UNITED KINGDOM
www.matt-clark.co.uk
6

Nick Clark
Sinister Flamingo Productions
606 High Street
Orillia, On L3V 6Y8
CANADA
Nicholasc@vfs.com
76

Krishnamurti M. Costa
San Clemente, California USA
www.antropus.com
8-15, [Front cover: CGChallenge
Machineflesh]

D

Paul Davidson
12 Beach Avenue,
Whitley Bay,
Tyne and Wear.
NE26 1EA
UNITED KINGDOM
krakenart@blueyonder.co.uk
75

Bernardo Delgado
Juan Rulfo #210
Jardines Vistahermosa,
cp28017 Colima MEXICO
30-37

Vincent Dubacq
Paris FRANCE
www.vincefx.com
vince.fx@libertysurf.fr
90

Jonny Duddle
Manchester
UNITED KINGDOM
jonny@duddlebug.co.uk
64

Richard Dumont
Montreal, Quebec. CANADA
www.fewlines.com
82

F

Pavel Fedorchuk
Onejskaya st 18,
Apartment 169,
Moscow 125438,
RUSSIAN FEDERATION
www.goldengrifon.ru
87

Nicolas Ferrand
UBISOFT
Montreal SPAIN\
www.redwhirlpool.com
90

David Freeman
Pixels and Potions
The Pixel Studios
4 Unity Street
BristolBS1 5HH
UNITED KINGDOM
www.pixelsandpotions.com
66

G

Roman Gunyavy (GURO)
guro@guro-games.com
http://guro-games.com
UKRAINE
84

J

Monsit Jangariyawong
THAILAND
monsitj@hotmail.com
74

Ian 'KingMob' Joyner
Blur Studio, 589 Venice Blvd, Venice,
California USA
ian@blur.com
6

K

Corlen K.
SOUTH AFRICA
corlenk@mweb.co.za
67

Alex Kaiser
Shipool Lodge, Innishannon
County Cork IRELAND
alexkaiser@gmail.com
74

Alena Klementeva
RUSSIAN FEDERATION
alena@digitalfun.ru
74

Rokas Klimavicius
LITHUANIA
dizon3d@yahoo.com
80

Sergey Korneev
RUSSIAN FEDERATION
sakor@aport.ru
70

L

Dave Lynch
California, USA
immorta25@aol.com
91

M

Michael Madic
California, USA
malandor@mindspring.com
60

Daryl Mandryk
Electronic Arts
Vancouver, CANADA
members.shaw.ca/dmandryk/
38-43

David Marsh
UNITED KINGDOM
dmarsh@climax.co.uk
81

Frederick Meier
DENMARK
frede_meier@hotmail.com
78-79

N

Eric Normandin
Bloom Digital Studio
CANADA
Cygnusx@videotron.ca
70

O

Marek Okon
Toronto CANADA
www.markokon.com
93

P

Christopher Page
11 Tandridge Drive
Orpington, Kent BR6 8BY
UNITED KINGDOM
cwpage@hotmail.com
80

Gary Pate
Sydney AUSTRALIA
www.ionization.net
72

Greg Petchkovsky
Sydney AUSTRALIA
www.gregpetch3d.com
16-23

Shawn Alan Peters
1409 South Lamar #242
Dallas, TX 75215 USA
www.shawnalanpeters.com
69

Friedric Petrequin
Heavydarkness Studio
2, rue Hector Berlioz
25700 Valentigney FRANCE
www.heavydarkness.com
76

Mike Phillips
BreakAway Games
4827 Plank Rd. Stewartstown,
PA, 17363 USA
www.mikephillips.ca
70

Andrzej Poturalski
Tuchola, Kujawsko-pomorskie
POLAND
damaged@artist.pl
84

R

Teemu Rajala
Niemenkyläntie 235
66320 Jurva
FINLAND
tepox80@hotmail.com
http://koti.mbnet.fi/~tepox/
84

Brian J. Read
14 Merville Ave, Te Atatu South,
Auckland, NEW ZEALAND
b.read@joice.net
77

Jeff Rey
FRANCE
jeff_atlanticus@yahoo.fr
44-49

Norman Rosenstech
FRANCE
norman.rosenstech.free.fr
62-63

Udom Ruangpaisitporn
Kantana Animation Co.,Ltd.
Bangkok THAILAND
tucker_3d@hotmail.com
72

S

Martin Sen
Brain and Bobo
SOUTH AFRICA
smartymarts@hotmail.com
70

Ila Soleimani
Tehran, IRAN
ila_solomon@yahoo.com
www.ilasolomon.com
24-29

T

Daniel Trbovic
SERBIA AND MONTENEGRO
danieldescartes@yahoo.com
60

Francis Tsai
San Diego, CA, USA
tsai@teamgt.com
www.teamgt.com
54-59

U

Panu Uomala
Bugbear Entertainment, Ltd
FINLAND
panu.uomala@bugbear.fi
83

V

Pablo Valbuena
SPAIN
www.p4b10.com
76

Yvan Verhoeven
BELGIUM
yvan.verhoeven@belgacom.net
73

Yura Vranchan
RUSSIAN FEDERATION
wizard2d@yandex.ru
85

Y

Ivelin Yordanov
BULGARIA
www.tripleart-bg.com
61

SOFTWARE INDEX

Products credited by popular name in this book are listed alphabetically here by company.

Adobe	Photoshop	www.adobe.com
Alias	Maya	www.alias.com
cebas	finalRender	www.finalrender.com
Chaos Group	VRay	www.vrayrender.com
Corel	Painter	www.vrayrender.com
Digimation	Shag Hair	www.digimation.com
discreet	3ds max	www.discreet.com
discreet	flame	www.discreet.com
eyeon Software	Digital Fusion	www.eyeonline.com
MAXON	BodyPaint	www.maxoncomputer.com
MAXON	CINEMA 4D	www.maxoncomputer.com
mentalimages	mental ray	www.mentalimages.com
NewTek	LightWave 3D	www.newtek.com
Pixologic	ZBrush	www.pixologic.com
Right Hemisphere	Deep Paint	www.righthemisphere.com
Softimage	SOFTIMAGE|XSI	www.softimage.com
Splutterfish	Brazil r/s	www.splutterfish.com

CG CHALLENGE XVI
GRAND SPACE OPERA
ICONS OF GALACTIC CIVILIZATION AND CONFLICT

Think big—really, really big! The Grand Space Opera Challenge, run 18 October 2004 - 17 January 2005 on CGNetworks.com tested artists to create iconic imagery that captured a pivotal moment in a vast galactic-spanning civilization. A civilization so vast that the only thread holding it together is a shared legacy of common legends. Legends of heroes, of heroic battles won against unimaginable odds, of crushing defeats and enemies that swarm through entire galaxies. Legends of utopian worlds, of vast planetary cities, of whole suns enclosed. Legends of secret sects and empire-spanning conspiracies. Legends of oppression and abject poverty. Legends of artists, of scientists, of religious leaders, of political leaders.

Coming soon to Ballistic Publishing is the Grand Space Opera book, featuring Making-Of tutorials from the winning artwork (2D and 3D) and a gallery of the stunning images emerging from this epic challenge. The distinguished panel of judges for the Grand Space Opera Challenge include: Stephan Martiniere (Star Wars: Episode 2 & 3); Iain McCaig (Star Wars: Episode 1, 2 & 3); Syd Mead (Blade Runner); Philip Straub (Senior Concept Artist, Electronic Arts); and Feng Zhu (Star Wars: Episode 3).

The Grand Space Opera Challenge is proudly sponsored by: Boxx Technologies; PNY Technologies; Softimage; Discreet; ART VPS; The Gnomon Workshop; Ballistic Publishing; Turbo Squid; Luxology; Pixologic; Corel; and Digital Tutors.

Don't miss the Grand Space Opera book, available 2nd Quarter 2005 from BallisticPublishing.com or authorized resellers.

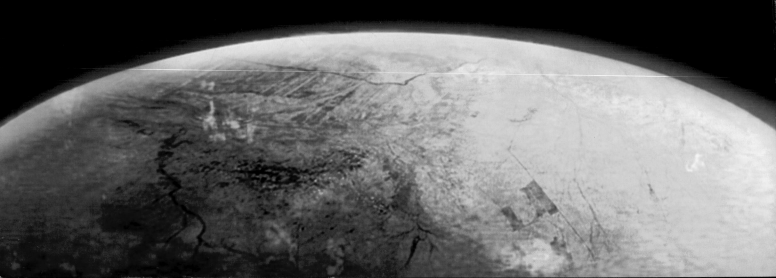